GREAT
BARBECUES

CONTENTS

Library of Congress Catalog Card Number: 88-062895

ISBN: 0-88176-433-7

This edition published by:
Publications International, Ltd.
7373 N. Cicero Avenue
Lincolnwood, IL 60646

Pictured on the back cover, clockwise from top left: Salmon Steaks in Orange-Honey Marinade *(see page 78)*, Fajitas with Pico de Gallo Sauce *(see page 11)*, Dan D's Chicken BBQ *(see page 54)* and Stuffed Cheese Burgers *(see page 40)*.

ACKNOWLEDGMENTS

The Kingsford Products Company would like to thank the following companies and organizations for the use of their recipes and photographs:

Alaska Seafood Marketing Institute, Salmon Division
American Lamb Council, Inc.
Beef Industry Council
California Apricot Advisory Board
California Beef Council
California Strawberry Advisory Board
California Tree Fruit Agreement

The Catfish Institute
National Broiler Council
National Fisheries Institute
National Hot Dog & Sausage Council
National Live Stock & Meat Board
National Turkey Federation
The Potato Board
Weber-Stephen Products Co.

Printed and bound in Yugoslavia
h g f e d c b a

HOT OFF THE GRILL

TO BARBECUE LOVERS EVERYWHERE

Kingsford's Great Barbecues *is all about sensational barbecues, from easy crowd-pleasing favorites to elegant grilled suppers. If you're new to the world of authentic charcoal cooking, we've included all the basics for starting off like a pro. And for the experienced outdoor chef, we offer plenty of intriguing menus to keep your grill fired up all summer—and winter—long!*

These mouth-watering recipes are all cooked over charcoal briquets—the heat of choice for 70% of grill owners. The reason charcoal is preferred for outdoor cooking is simple. It's the real wood char in briquets that helps deliver the rich, smoky flavor we associate with the true taste of barbecue.

*We've even settled the controversy about which fire—charcoal or gas—grills a better burger. Results of controlled taste tests from across the country show the hands-down winner is the charcoal-grilled burger—ranked **number one** by the majority of tasters for best barbecued flavor.*

Barbecuing may be synonymous with summer, but many outdoor cooks are discovering what passionate grill enthusiasts have known all along. Winter barbecue is a sensation. Discover how easy it is to barbecue a golden holiday turkey (see the recipe on page 64) and get ready to start a new family tradition. Turkey never tasted so good.

From our family to yours, here's to a great year of great barbecues!

Sandy Sullivan and the Kingsford BBQ Pros

A DASH OF HISTORY

Henry Ford gets credit for more than the Model T. His ingenuity is responsible for launching America's passion for outdoor cooking. You might say he's the original baron of barbecue—all because he couldn't tolerate waste.

In the early 1900s, Ford operated a northern Michigan sawmill that made wooden framing for his Model Ts. He looked on in frustration at the growing piles of wood scraps and wondered how they could be put to productive use. He came up with the idea to chip the wood into small pieces, convert it to charcoal, grind it into powder, then compress it into the now-familiar pillow-shaped briquets. These convenient briquets were originally sold through Ford automobile agencies.

Ford put his brother-in-law, E.G. Kingsford, in charge of the charcoal operation. Together, they helped make barbecuing an American tradition. Ford Charcoal, later named **Kingsford**® charcoal briquets, is the original and still the number one brand sold in the nation today.

WHAT TYPE OF CHARCOAL?

Successful barbecuing starts with a good fire. Premium quality briquets, like **Kingsford**® charcoal, help deliver a perfect fire three ways. They light quicker so the coals are ready sooner. They burn more evenly to produce balanced heat, and they perform consistently—bag after bag. The renewed interest in authentic charcoal cooking has spawned extra convenience and new flavor in the types of charcoal available.

Instant Lighting Charcoal Briquets. An especially good choice for midweek barbecues when time is at a premium. Products like **Match light**® charcoal briquets already contain just the right amount of lighter fluid to produce a quick-starting fire. Simply stack the briquets into a pyramid and light several briquets with a match. The coals will be ready in about 20 minutes. Be sure to close the bag tightly after each use.

Charcoal Briquets with Mesquite Wood Chips. The perfect selection for cooks who enjoy the wonderful flavor of mesquite but feel less comfortable

grilling over pure mesquite charcoal, which burns hotter and less evenly. For example, **Kingsford® with Mesquite** charcoal briquets are compressed charcoal briquets with mesquite chips blended into them. These briquets produce real mesquite smoke to enhance the flavor of outdoor fare.

It's important to remember that charcoal is porous and will absorb moisture. Always store briquets in a dry area, and keep the bag in a tightly closed or covered container. Charcoal that has been exposed to humidity or moisture can be more difficult to light.

SAFETY FIRST

Make sure the grill is on a solid surface and is set away from shrubbery, grass and overhangs. NEVER use gasoline or kerosene as a lighter fluid starter. Either one can cause an explosion. To get a sluggish fire going, *do not add lighter fluid directly to hot coals.* Instead, take 2 to 3 additional briquets, place them in a small metal container and add lighter fluid. When the briquets have absorbed the lighter fluid (1 to 2 minutes), add them to the pyramid of briquets, then light with a match. These briquets will restart the fire.

Remember that coals are hot—up to 1000°F—and that the heat transfers to the barbecue grill, grid, tools and food. Always wear fireproof mitts when cooking and handling grill and tools.

BUILDING PERFECT FIRES

How Much Charcoal? A 5-pound bag of **Kingsford®** charcoal contains 75 to 90 briquets; a 10-pound bag between 150 and 180; and a 20-pound bag 300 to 360 briquets. The number of briquets required for barbecuing depends on the size and type of grill and the amount of food to be prepared. Weather conditions also have an effect; strong winds, very cold temperatures or highly humid conditions increase the number of briquets needed for a good fire. As a rule of thumb, it takes about 30 briquets to grill 1 pound of meat. For example, you'll need 45 briquets to grill six 4-ounce hamburgers.

For grilling meat directly over the coals, you want enough charcoal—in a single layer—to extend 1 to 2 inches beyond the area of the food on the grill. Pour briquets into the grill unit to determine the quantity needed, then stack them into a pyramid.

When cooking in a covered grill using an indirect method, food is placed over a drip pan and the coals are banked either to one side or on both sides of the pan. This method is recommended for large cuts of meat (like roasts) and for fatty meats to eliminate flame flare-ups. Here's how to determine the number of briquets needed:

BRIQUETS NEEDED FOR INDIRECT COOKING, COVERED GRILL				
	Diameter of Grill (inches)			
	26¾	22½	18½	14
Briquets needed each side of drip pan for cooking 45 to 50 minutes	30	25	16	15
Briquets to be added on each side of drip pan every 45 minutes	9	8	5	4

Using Lighter Fluid. Stack briquets into a pyramid. Soak briquets with at least ½ cup lighter fluid, like **Kingsford™ Odorless charcoal lighter.** Wait 1 minute to allow fluid to soak into briquets. Then light with a match. Coals will be ready in 20 to 30 minutes, when they are about 80% ashed over. At night, they will have a noticeable cheery glow.

Using a Chimney Starter. This method is essentially failure-proof and no lighter fluid is required. First, remove the grid from the grill and set the chimney starter in the base of the grill. Then crumple a couple of sheets of newspaper and place them in the bottom portion of the chimney starter. Fill the top portion with charcoal briquets. Light the newspaper. Do not disturb the starter; coals will be ready in 20 to 30 minutes. Be sure to wear fireproof mitts when emptying coals from the chimney starter into the base of the grill.

Using an Electric Starter. Nestle the electric starter in the coals. Then plug the starter into a heavy-duty extension cord. Plug the cord into the nearest available outlet. After 8 to 10 minutes, when ash begins to form on the briquets, unplug the starter, remove it, and carefully set it aside. Arrange the briquets in a single layer, close together.

How Hot is the Grill? If you don't have a grill thermometer, here is a quick, easy way to estimate the temperature on the grill surface. Hold your hand, palm-side-down, just above the grid. Count "one thousand one, one thousand two," etc., until the heat is uncomfortable. If you can keep your hand in place before pulling away:

- 2 seconds—it's a hot fire, about 375°F or more.
- 3 seconds—it's a medium-hot fire, about 350° to 375°F.
- 4 seconds—it's a medium fire, about 300° to 350°F.
- 5 seconds—it's a low fire, about 200° to 300°F.

FLAVORED SMOKE

Flavored smoke, enriched with heady aromas from hardwoods and fresh or dried herbs, is the latest sensation in barbecue flavorings. Outdoor cooks find it's both easy and fun to experiment with different meats and flavor combinations. Here are some suggestions for getting started:

As a general rule, a little goes a long way. Added flavorings should complement, not overpower, food's natural taste. Always soak flavorings, such as wood chunks, wood chips or herbs, in water at least 30 minutes before adding to the coals. You want the flavorings to smolder and smoke, not burn.

Hickory and mesquite chips or wood chunks are the most readily available flavorings. Other good choices are oak (good with heartier meats), cherry or apple wood (flavorful companions to poultry) and alder wood from the Northwest (marvelous with fish). Look for **Kingsford® Heart-O-Hickory smoke chips** in your store's barbecue section.

Grapevine cuttings and even shells from nuts like almonds, pecans or walnuts add interesting flavor. You can also try water-soaked garlic cloves and orange or lemon peels.

Small bunches of fresh or dried herbs, soaked in water, can add fragrant flavor as well. Rosemary, bay leaves, oregano and tarragon, for example, can be teamed with wood chips or simply used by themselves.

DRY RUBS AND MARINADES

Dry rubs are combinations of seasonings and spices rubbed onto meat before grilling. Basic rubs often include coarsely ground black or white pepper, paprika and garlic powder. Some include mustard and brown sugar—even cayenne pepper. Crushed herbs are other good choices—sage, basil, thyme and oregano, for example.

Marinades, like dry rubs, add flavor, but they also help tenderize less tender cuts of meat. Basic marinades include an acidic ingredient responsible for tenderizing—generally from wine, vinegar, soy sauce or lemon juice—combined with herbs, seasonings and oil. Fish and vegetables don't usually need tenderizing and should be marinated for only short periods of time (no more than a few hours). Beef, pork, lamb and chicken all benefit from being marinated for a few hours to overnight. Use leftover marinades as a baste while cooking. You can also serve leftover marinades as a sauce. However, follow food safety practices by boiling the marinade for a few minutes before serving.

A WORD ABOUT SAUCES

Sauces, rich and thick with tomato, or savory with garlic, onion and spices, add delicious flavor to almost any grilled fare. Premium sauces, like **K.C. Masterpiece®** barbecue sauce, capture real homemade taste and are a barbecue staple worth using often. Serve warmed sauce on the side for added zest. Here's how to protect the rich, deep color and spicy flavor of barbecue sauce, especially tomato- and molasses-based ones that can burn if applied too early:

- For grilled steaks and chops: Baste with sauce after meat has been turned for the last time, about the last 3 minutes of grilling.
- For grilled chicken: Baste with sauce the last 10 minutes; turn once.
- For hot dogs and sausage: Baste with sauce the last 5 to 6 minutes.
- For barbecued meats (cooked by indirect method): Baste with sauce the last hour of cooking.
- For smoked meats: Baste with sauce the last 30 to 45 minutes.

BARBECUE TIPS

- To keep food from sticking to the grid and make it easy to turn, rub the grid with vegetable oil before cooking.
- Always use tongs or a spatula when handling meat. Piercing meat with a fork allows delicious juices to escape and makes meat less moist.
- When making kabobs, if you use wooden or bamboo skewers, be sure to soak them in cold water 20 minutes before using.
- The secret to evenly cooked vegetable and meat kabobs is to parboil solid or starchy vegetables before they are threaded onto skewers for grilling.
- Foods wrapped in foil and cooked on the grill should be turned often to prevent burning and assure even cooking.
- When barbecuing food for more than 45 minutes, add 10 to 12 briquets around the outer edge of the fire as cooking starts. When these briquets are ready, add them to the center of the fire as needed to maintain constant temperature.

REGIONAL BARBECUES

America loves to barbecue. Featured here are favorites from all over the United States, including chili-pepper-stuffed chicken, smoked grilled salmon and succulent sauce-laden ribs. Suggested menus offer you great ideas for serving complete meals.

BUTTERFLIED LEG OF LAMB

Makes 8 to 10 servings

1 boneless leg of lamb (6 pounds), butterflied
½ cup olive or vegetable oil
½ cup chopped fresh mint *or* 2 tablespoons dried
    mint, crushed
2 cloves garlic, minced
4 teaspoons Dijon-style mustard
1 tablespoon black peppercorns, cracked
1 tablespoon chopped fresh rosemary *or*
    1 teaspoon dried rosemary, crushed
1½ teaspoons finely shredded lemon peel

Remove excess fat and thin fat covering from surface of lamb. With meat mallet, pound meat to even thickness, about 1½ inches. Place lamb in large plastic bag. Place bag in shallow roasting pan. In small bowl, combine remaining ingredients; pour over lamb in bag. Close bag; refrigerate 2 to 5 days, turning occasionally.

Arrange medium-hot **Kingsford® briquets** around drip pan. Drain meat; reserve marinade. Put 2 skewers diagonally through meat to keep flat while grilling. Insert meat thermometer in thickest part of meat. Place lamb over drip pan. Cover grill and cook until thermometer registers 140°F for rare (35 to 40 minutes), 160°F for medium (about 45 minutes). Brush with marinade often. Turn meat once halfway through cooking time. Remove meat; let stand, covered, 15 minutes. Carve meat into thin slices to serve.

Northeast Barbecued Lamb Dinner:
Butterflied Leg of Lamb with
Grill-Roasted Onions and Vegetable-Rice Salad
(recipes on page 8)

Northeast Barbecued Lamb Dinner

- **Skewered Shrimp with Lemon**
- **Butterflied Leg of Lamb**
- **Grill-Roasted Onions**
- **Vegetable-Rice Salad**
- **Strawberry Lemondrift Pie**

To prepare this menu, you'll need to use 75 Kingsford® Charcoal Briquets (about 5 pounds).

GRILL-ROASTED ONIONS

Makes 8 servings

4 medium yellow onions, unpeeled
1 tablespoon olive or vegetable oil
  Salt and pepper
8 teaspoons butter or margarine

Cut unpeeled onion into halves lengthwise. Brush onions with oil. Place onion halves on 18×18-inch piece of heavy-duty foil. Season to taste with salt and pepper. Place 1 teaspoon butter on each onion half. Wrap loosely in foil; seal edges tightly.

Grill packet, on covered grill, over medium-hot **Kingsford® briquets** 20 minutes or until onions are tender, turning packet once. Unwrap packet and serve onions in skins.

VEGETABLE-RICE SALAD

Makes 8 servings

3 cups cooked long grain rice
1¾ cups prepared Hidden Valley Ranch® Original Ranch® Salad Dressing
2 medium tomatoes, chopped
  Milk
  Lettuce
  Cooked green beans (optional)

In bowl, combine rice and salad dressing. Toss gently to coat. Cover; refrigerate. Just before serving, stir in tomatoes. Stir in 2 to 3 tablespoons milk if rice mixture seems dry. Turn into lettuce-lined salad bowl. Garnish with green beans and additional chopped tomato, if desired.

SKEWERED SHRIMP WITH LEMON

Makes 8 appetizer servings

16 fresh or frozen large shrimp, shelled and deveined
½ cup olive or vegetable oil
2 lemons
½ cup fine dry bread crumbs
½ teaspoon pepper

Thaw shrimp, if frozen. Thread 2 shrimp on each of 8 skewers. Brush with 2 tablespoons of the oil. With vegetable peeler, remove peel from lemons; shred finely. In bowl, combine lemon peel, bread crumbs and ¼ teaspoon of the pepper. Press crumb mixture firmly onto shrimp to coat evenly. Refrigerate until ready to grill.

For dipping sauce, squeeze juice from lemons (you should have about 6 tablespoons juice). Combine juice with remaining 6 tablespoons oil and remaining ¼ teaspoon pepper; set aside.

Grill breaded shrimp, on covered grill, over medium-hot **Kingsford® briquets** 4 minutes. Turn skewers; grill 4 minutes longer or until shrimp are pink and crumbs are slightly browned. Serve shrimp with lemony dipping sauce.

STRAWBERRY LEMONDRIFT PIE

Makes 6 to 8 servings

2 pints fresh strawberries
½ cup milk
1 envelope unflavored gelatin
⅔ cup granulated sugar
1½ tablespoons grated lemon peel
¼ cup fresh lemon juice
2 cups whipping cream
1 baked and cooled 9-inch pie shell
  Confectioners' sugar

Remove stems from strawberries. Place strawberries in bowl; cover and refrigerate. In 1-quart saucepan, combine milk and gelatin; set aside 5 minutes. Stir in sugar. Stir over low heat until gelatin and sugar are completely dissolved. Stir in lemon peel and juice. Cool to room temperature. Refrigerate until mixture is syrupy, about 15 minutes. Whip cream in large mixer bowl until stiff. Fold in gelatin mixture. Spoon into pie shell, mounding top. Cut strawberries into halves; cover pie with strawberries. Chill until firm, about 2 hours. Dust top lightly with confectioners' sugar before serving.

*Recipe courtesy of **California Strawberry Advisory Board***

Tex-Mex Barbecue Dinner

- Nachos
- Avocado-Tomato Salad
- Fajitas with Pico de Gallo Sauce
- Grilled Potatoes
- Blue Ribbon Pinto Beans
- Texas Pecan Pralines (see page 30)

To prepare this menu, you'll need to use 50 Kingsford® Charcoal Briquets (about 3 pounds).

NACHOS

Makes 8 servings

1 bag (8 ounces) tortilla chips
1 can (16 ounces) refried beans
   Pickled jalapeño pepper strips (about 24)
2 cups shredded Monterey Jack or Cheddar
   cheese (about 8 ounces)

Place half the tortilla chips in large iron skillet. Spoon half the beans over chips and arrange jalapeño strips on top. Sprinkle with half the cheese. Make a second layer with remaining ingredients. Grill, on covered grill, over medium-hot **Kingsford® briquets** 6 to 8 minutes or until cheese melts.

AVOCADO-TOMATO SALAD

Makes 8 servings

2 ripe large avocados, seeded and peeled
   Lemon juice
2 or 3 medium tomatoes
   Lettuce leaves
   Prepared Hidden Valley Ranch® Original Ranch®
   Salad Dressing

Slice avocados and sprinkle with lemon juice to prevent browning. Cut tomatoes into wedges. Arrange avocado slices and tomato wedges on individual lettuce-lined salad plates. Drizzle with salad dressing.

GRILLED POTATOES

Makes 8 servings

6 medium potatoes
⅓ cup olive or vegetable oil
¾ teaspoon salt
½ teaspoon garlic powder
¼ teaspoon pepper

Peel potatoes, if desired, and cut each into 4 wedges. In large bowl, combine oil, salt, garlic powder and pepper. Add potatoes; toss to coat. Wrap potatoes in heavy-duty foil; seal edges tightly. Grill packet, on covered grill, not directly over medium-hot **Kingsford® briquets** about 35 minutes or until potatoes are tender.

BLUE RIBBON PINTO BEANS

Makes 6 to 8 servings

2 pounds dried pinto beans
1 pound sliced smoked bacon, cut into 1-inch
   pieces
2 medium tomatoes, diced
1½ tablespoons ground cumin
1½ tablespoons chili powder
2 garlic cloves, minced
1 jalapeño or serrano chili pepper, minced
   Salt

Place beans in large heavy saucepan. Cover with water and bring to boil. Drain. Return beans to saucepan. Add enough water to cover by 2 to 3 inches. Add remaining ingredients except salt. Bring mixture to boil. Reduce heat to low and simmer about 3½ hours or until beans are very soft, adding more water as necessary to keep beans submerged. Season to taste with salt and cook 15 minutes longer, uncovered, if liquid is thin.

FAJITAS

Makes 8 servings

2 pounds beef skirt steak or flank steak
¾ cup beer
½ cup lime juice
2 tablespoons Worcestershire sauce
8 flour tortillas (6-inch)
Pico de Gallo Sauce (recipe follows)

Trim excess fat from steak. In shallow glass dish, combine beer, lime juice and Worcestershire sauce. Add steak; turn to coat with marinade. Cover and refrigerate overnight, spooning marinade over meat occasionally.

Drain steak; reserve marinade. Pat steak dry with paper toweling. Grill steak, on covered grill, over medium-hot **Kingsford®** briquets 8 to 10 minutes, basting meat occasionally with marinade. Turn and grill to desired doneness, allowing 8 to 10 minutes longer for medium. Carve meat across grain into thin slices.

Meanwhile, wrap tortillas in large piece of heavy-duty foil; place tortillas at edge of grill 5 minutes or until heated through. Wrap steak slices in warmed tortillas; top with chilled Pico de Gallo Sauce.

PICO DE GALLO SAUCE

Makes about 1¾ cups

3 medium tomatoes, peeled and chopped
½ cup chopped green onions
1 large fresh Anaheim chili pepper, seeded and chopped
1 fresh jalapeño pepper, seeded and chopped
2 teaspoons chopped fresh cilantro or parsley
1 teaspoon salt

In small bowl, combine tomatoes, onions, peppers, cilantro and salt. Cover and refrigerate 5 hours or overnight.

Tex-Mex Barbecue Dinner:
Fajitas with Pico de Gallo Sauce;
Avocado-Tomato Salad and Nachos
(recipes on page 9)

Southeast Pork Barbecue

- **Barbecued Pork Leg with Sam's Mop Sauce**
- **Southern-Style Squash and Okra**
- **Saucy New Potatoes**
- **Corn Muffins**
- **Peaches in Port**

To prepare this menu, you'll need to use about 134 Kingsford® Charcoal Briquets (about 8 pounds).

CORN MUFFINS

Makes about 14 muffins

1 cup all-purpose flour
1 cup yellow cornmeal
¼ cup sugar
4 teaspoons baking powder
¾ teaspoon salt
2 eggs
1 cup milk
¼ cup vegetable oil or melted shortening

In bowl, stir together flour, cornmeal, sugar, baking powder and salt. Add eggs, milk and oil. Beat just until combined; do not overbeat.

Grease muffin cups or line with paper baking cups; fill two-thirds full. Bake in 400°F oven 15 to 20 minutes or until done. Let stand 3 minutes in pan. Loosen muffins; remove from pan.

SAUCY NEW POTATOES

Makes 4 to 6 servings

1½ pounds new potatoes
½ cup K.C. Masterpiece® Hickory Barbecue Sauce
¼ cup water
Salt and pepper

Cut largest potatoes in half; arrange on 18×18-inch piece of heavy-duty foil. In small bowl, combine barbecue sauce and water; pour over potatoes. Season to taste with salt and pepper. Fold foil over potatoes; seal edges tightly. Grill packet, on covered grill, over medium-hot **Kingsford®** briquets about 30 minutes or until potatoes are tender. Turn packet over after 15 minutes.

BARBECUED PORK LEG

Makes about 20 servings

  1 boneless pork leg roast, rolled and tied (8 to
     10 pounds)
    Sam's Mop Sauce (recipe follows)
    K.C. Masterpiece® Hickory Barbecue Sauce

Arrange medium-hot **Kingsford® briquets** around drip pan. Place prepared pork leg over drip pan; cover grill and cook pork 4 to 4½ hours (adding additional briquets as necessary) or until meat thermometer inserted in thickest portion registers 170°F. Baste pork with Sam's Mop Sauce every 30 minutes, patting a thin coating of sauce on meat with cotton swab mop or pastry brush. Let stand, covered with foil, 10 minutes before serving.

Meanwhile, in saucepan, combine remaining Mop Sauce with an equal amount of barbecue sauce; bring to boil. Slice pork and serve with sauce mixture.

SAM'S MOP SAUCE

Makes 2¼ cups

  1 lemon
  1 cup water
  1 cup cider vinegar
  1 tablespoon butter or margarine
  1 tablespoon olive or vegetable oil
 ½ teaspoon cayenne pepper
 1½ to 3 teaspoons hot pepper sauce
 1½ to 3 teaspoons Worcestershire sauce
 1½ teaspoons black pepper

With vegetable peeler, remove peel from lemon; squeeze juice from lemon. In heavy saucepan, combine lemon peel, juice and remaining ingredients. Bring to boil. Place saucepan on grill to keep warm, if space permits.

SOUTHERN-STYLE SQUASH AND OKRA

Makes 4 to 6 servings

  2 small onions, sliced and separated into rings
  3 medium crookneck squash, cut into ¼-inch
     slices
  1 package (10 ounces) frozen whole okra, thawed
     and cut into bite-size pieces
  2 tablespoons butter or margarine
  1 clove garlic, minced
  1 teaspoon salt
 ⅛ teaspoon pepper
 ½ teaspoon dried thyme, crushed
  1 tablespoon lemon juice
 ¼ cup grated Cheddar cheese (1 ounce)

Place onion slices, squash and okra on 24×18-inch piece of heavy-duty foil. Dot with butter. Sprinkle with garlic, salt, pepper, thyme and lemon juice. Fold and seal foil edges tightly. Grill packet, on covered grill, over medium-hot **Kingsford® briquets** 25 to 30 minutes or until tender, turning packet over once. To serve, unwrap foil packet and sprinkle with Cheddar cheese.

PEACHES IN PORT

Makes 4 to 6 servings

  6 to 8 large fresh peaches, peeled and cut into
     sixths
  2 teaspoons lemon juice
 ¼ cup tawny port wine
  2 tablespoons butter or margarine

Arrange peaches on 24×18-inch piece of heavy-duty foil. Sprinkle with lemon juice and port; dot with butter. Fold foil loosely around fruit and seal edges tightly. Grill packet, on covered grill, over medium-hot **Kingsford® briquets** about 15 minutes or until fruit is hot, turning packet once.

Southeast Pork Barbecue:
*Corn Muffins (page 11), Peaches in Port
and Barbecued Pork Leg with Sam's Mop Sauce*

East Coast Fish and Oyster Barbecue

- Grilled Swordfish
- Grilled Tomatoes
- Savoy Cabbage Pockets
- Grilled Potato Hash (see page 19)
- White Zinfandel wine

To prepare this menu, you'll need to use 60 Kingsford® Charcoal Briquets (about 4 pounds).

SAVOY CABBAGE POCKETS

Makes 4 servings

8 to 12 savoy cabbage leaves or green cabbage leaves
¼ cup olive or vegetable oil
1 pint shucked oysters
1 tablespoon chopped fresh thyme *or* 1 teaspoon dried thyme, crushed
Salt and pepper

Immerse cabbage leaves in large saucepan of boiling water 3 minutes; drain. Remove center vein. Brush cabbage leaves with 2 tablespoons of the oil. Divide oysters among cabbage leaves; lightly sprinkle with thyme, salt and pepper.

Roll up leaves, jelly-roll style, folding in sides. Brush outer leaves with remaining 2 tablespoons oil. Place in foil pan, seam-side down. Place uncovered foil pan on grill not directly over coals. Cover grill; cook over medium-hot **Kingsford®** briquets 10 to 15 minutes or until oysters are firm and edges curled.

GRILLED SWORDFISH

Makes 4 servings

4 fresh or frozen swordfish steaks, ½ inch thick (about 2 pounds)
⅓ cup tomato paste (half of 6-ounce can)
¼ cup dry red wine
6 cloves garlic, sliced
⅛ teaspoon cayenne pepper or few dashes hot pepper sauce
3 tablespoons chopped cilantro or parsley
2 tablespoons olive or vegetable oil

Thaw fish, if frozen. In small saucepan, combine tomato paste, wine, garlic and cayenne. Bring to boil. Reduce heat; simmer, covered, 1 hour, stirring occasionally. Press mixture through sieve; discard garlic. Stir in cilantro and oil. Cool to room temperature.

Place fish in shallow glass dish; brush cooled marinade over fish. Cover and refrigerate 30 minutes.

Drain fish; reserve marinade. Grill fish, on covered grill, over medium-hot **Kingsford®** briquets 4 minutes; brush with marinade. Turn and cook 3 to 5 minutes longer or until fish flakes easily when tested with fork. Brush again with marinade. Transfer to serving platter.

GRILLED TOMATOES

Makes 4 servings

2 large tomatoes
2 tablespoons olive or vegetable oil
1½ teaspoons chopped fresh basil *or* ½ teaspoon dried basil, crushed
Salt and pepper

In covered grill, arrange medium-hot **Kingsford®** briquets on one side of grill. Slice each tomato in half crosswise; remove excess juice and seeds. Drizzle tomato halves with oil. Place in foil pan. Place foil pan on edge of grill not directly over coals. (Swordfish steaks will grill directly over coals.) Cook tomatoes, on covered grill, 10 to 14 minutes or until heated through. Sprinkle cut surfaces with basil, salt and pepper. Garnish with fresh basil, if desired.

East Coast Fish and Oyster Barbecue:
Grilled Tomatoes, Savoy Cabbage Pockets and Grilled Swordfish

Northwest Grilled Cornish Game Hen Dinner

- Grilled Cornish Game Hens
- Rice Pilaf with Sauteed Pecans
- Skewered Vegetables
- Baked Honey Apples

To prepare this menu, you'll need to use 65 Kingsford® Charcoal Briquets (about 4 pounds).

RICE PILAF WITH SAUTEED PECANS

Makes 4 servings

⅓ cup wild rice
2⅔ cups water
1 teaspoon instant chicken bouillon granules
1 cup long grain rice
½ cup coarsely chopped pecans
3 tablespoons butter or margarine
2 tablespoons chopped parsley

Wash wild rice under cold running water in strainer about 1 minute, lifting rice to rinse well.

In 2-quart saucepan with tight-fitting lid, combine water, wild rice and chicken bouillon granules. Bring to boil. Reduce heat; cover and simmer 20 minutes. Add long grain rice; return to boil. Reduce heat and simmer, covered, 20 to 25 minutes longer or until rice is tender and water is absorbed.

Meanwhile, in small skillet, saute pecans in butter about 2 minutes or until golden. Add pecans to hot rice mixture; stir in parsley. Toss lightly until combined. Serve immediately.

BAKED HONEY APPLES

Makes 4 servings

2 to 3 apples, cored and sliced into ¾-inch rings
½ cup butter or margarine
⅓ cup honey

Arrange 2 or 3 apple rings on each of four 12×12-inch pieces of heavy-duty foil. Dot with butter; drizzle with honey. Fold foil loosely around apples; seal edges. Grill packets, on covered grill, over medium-hot Kingsford® briquets 12 to 15 minutes or until apples are crisp-tender, turning packets once.

GRILLED CORNISH GAME HENS

Makes 4 servings

2 Cornish game hens (1 to 1½ pounds each)
3 tablespoons olive or vegetable oil
⅓ cup lemon juice
1 tablespoon black peppercorns, coarsely crushed
½ teaspoon salt
   Sprig fresh rosemary

Split hens lengthwise. Rinse under cold running water; pat dry with paper toweling. Place hens in large plastic bag; set in bowl. In small bowl, combine oil, lemon juice, peppercorns and salt. Pour marinade over hens in bag. Close bag securely and refrigerate several hours or overnight, turning hens occasionally to coat with marinade.

Arrange medium-hot Kingsford® briquets around drip pan. Just before grilling, add rosemary sprig to coals. Drain hens; reserve marinade. Place hens, skin-side up, over drip pan. Cover grill and cook 45 minutes or until thigh moves easily and juices run clear. Baste with marinade occasionally. Garnish with fresh rosemary, if desired.

SKEWERED VEGETABLES

Makes 4 servings

2 medium zucchini, cut into 1½-inch slices
8 small boiling onions
8 fresh medium mushrooms
2 tablespoons butter or margarine, melted
4 cherry tomatoes
   Salt and pepper

In medium saucepan, cook zucchini and onions, covered, in boiling water to cover for 1 minute. Remove with slotted spoon and drain. Alternately thread zucchini, onions and mushrooms on 4 skewers. Brush with butter.

Grill vegetables, on covered grill, over medium-hot Kingsford® briquets 6 minutes or until tender, carefully turning skewers once. Add cherry tomatoes to end of skewers during last minute of grilling. Season to taste with salt and pepper. Serve immediately.

Northwest Grilled Cornish Game Hen Dinner:
Grilled Cornish Game Hens, Skewered Vegetables, Rice Pilaf with Sauteed Pecans and Baked Honey Apples

Southern Spicy Ribs and Fruit Dinner

- Pork Spareribs
- Hot Apple Salad
- Grilled Potato Hash
- Corn Muffins (see page 11)
- Fruit Kabobs with Whiskey Baste

To prepare this menu, you'll need to use 80 Kingsford® Charcoal Briquets (about 5 pounds).

PORK SPARERIBS

Makes 4 servings

4 pounds pork spareribs or pork back ribs
1¼ cups K.C. Masterpiece® Barbecue Sauce

Remove breast section from ribs, if desired. Cut ribs into 4 or 5 rib portions. Arrange medium-hot **Kingsford® briquets** around drip pan. Place ribs over drip pan; cover grill and cook 1¼ hours. Turn; brush with barbecue sauce. Cook, on covered grill, 10 to 15 minutes longer or until ribs are thoroughly cooked, brushing once or twice with barbecue sauce. Bring remaining sauce to boil and serve with ribs, if desired.

HOT APPLE SALAD

Makes 4 servings

2 red cooking apples, cored and thinly sliced (2 cups)
3 cups finely shredded red cabbage
4 teaspoons butter or margarine, cut up
3 tablespoons rice wine vinegar
4 teaspoons sugar
¾ teaspoon salt
¼ teaspoon caraway seed

In bowl, toss together all ingredients. Turn out onto 24×18-inch piece of heavy-duty foil. Fold edges around apple mixture; seal edges tightly. Grill packet, on covered grill, over medium-hot **Kingsford® briquets** 45 minutes or until apples are tender, turning packet every 15 minutes.

Southern Spicy Ribs and Fruit Dinner:
Pork Spareribs, Fruit Kabobs with Whiskey Baste and Hot Apple Salad

GRILLED POTATO HASH

Makes 4 servings

2 tablespoons butter or margarine
2 tablespoons all-purpose flour
¾ teaspoon salt
¼ teaspoon seasoned pepper
⅛ teaspoon celery seed
1 cup milk
4 medium potatoes, peeled and cut into cubes
1 cup chopped onion
½ cup chopped green pepper
¼ teaspoon paprika

In medium saucepan, melt butter. Blend in flour, salt, seasoned pepper and celery seed. Stir in milk all at once. Cook and stir over medium heat until thickened and bubbly. Cook and stir 1 minute longer.

Add potatoes, onion and green pepper. Turn potato mixture out onto 24×18-inch piece of heavy-duty foil; sprinkle with paprika. Fold foil loosely around potato mixture and seal edges tightly.

Grill packet, on covered grill, over medium-hot **Kingsford® briquets** 45 to 50 minutes or until potatoes are tender, turning packet every 15 minutes.

FRUIT KABOBS WITH WHISKEY BASTE

Makes 4 servings

2 tablespoons honey
2 tablespoons whiskey
1 tablespoon lemon juice
1 can (8 ounces) pineapple chunks, drained
1 large banana, diagonally sliced into 1-inch pieces
1 orange, peeled and sectioned
8 maraschino cherries

In large bowl, combine honey, whiskey and lemon juice; add pineapple chunks, banana pieces, orange sections and cherries. Gently toss to coat fruit well. Cover and refrigerate up to 2 hours or until ready to grill.

Remove fruit with slotted spoon, reserving whiskey baste. Alternately thread fruit on skewers. Grill fruit kabobs, on covered grill, over medium-low **Kingsford® briquets** 5 to 10 minutes or until fruit is warmed through, basting frequently with whiskey baste.

Western Chestnuts and Tenderloin Barbecue

- Roasted Chestnuts
- Grilled Tenderloin with Cognac
- Garlic Mushrooms
- Creamy Potato Bake (see page 27)
- Fresh Blackberry Cobbler
- Burgundy Wine

To prepare this menu, you'll need to use 70 Kingsford® Charcoal Briquets (about 4½ pounds).

GRILLED TENDERLOIN WITH COGNAC

Makes 8 servings

1 beef tenderloin roast (2 pounds)
¼ cup whole green, white or black peppercorns
Garlic Mushrooms (recipe follows)
⅓ cup cognac or other brandy
1 cup whipping cream
2 tablespoons Dijon-style mustard
1 tablespoon Worcestershire sauce
2 teaspoons lemon juice

Trim excess fat from roast. Crack peppercorns coarsely with mortar and pestle; sprinkle on roast and press into surface.

Arrange medium-hot **Kingsford® briquets** around drip pan. Place roast over drip pan. Cover grill and cook, turning once, until meat thermometer registers 140°F for rare (about 45 minutes), 150°F for medium-rare (about 55 minutes), or 170°F for well-done (about 60 minutes). While roast is cooking, prepare Garlic Mushrooms. About 15 minutes before meat is done, place mushrooms next to meat.

When roast is grilled to desired doneness, warm cognac in skillet on range-top. Remove from heat. Place roast in heated skillet. Carefully ignite cognac with match; allow flames to subside, carefully spooning cognac over meat. Remove roast to serving platter; reserve juices.

In saucepan, combine cream, mustard and Worcestershire sauce. Bring to boil. Cook and stir, over medium-low heat, 3 minutes or until slightly thickened. Remove from heat; stir in lemon juice and reserved cognac juices. Carve roast and arrange with Garlic Mushrooms. Pour cream sauce over sliced roast and mushrooms. Garnish with fresh rosemary, if desired.

ROASTED CHESTNUTS

Makes 8 servings

4 cups chestnuts

Using sharp knife, make an × on flat side of each chestnut. Place nuts in 13×9×2-inch baking pan or in foil pan. Grill chestnuts, on covered grill, over medium-hot **Kingsford® briquets** 10 to 15 minutes or until skin begins to lift away from nuts, stirring once. Peel outer skin while still warm.

GARLIC MUSHROOMS

Makes 8 servings

32 large fresh mushrooms
½ cup olive or vegetable oil
2 cloves garlic, minced

Remove stems from mushrooms; reserve caps. In bowl, combine oil and garlic; add mushroom caps. Gently toss to coat. Remove mushrooms with slotted spoon; place mushroom caps on piece of heavy-duty foil. Seal edges tightly. Grill at side of roast over medium-hot **Kingsford® briquets** 10 to 15 minutes or until tender.

FRESH BLACKBERRY COBBLER

Makes 8 servings

4 cups whole blackberries or blueberries
½ cup sugar
2 tablespoons butter or margarine
1 cup packaged biscuit mix
2 tablespoons sugar
⅓ cup light cream
Vanilla ice cream

In 10-inch heavy skillet with tight-fitting lid, combine blackberries and ½ cup sugar. Dot with butter. Cook and stir, over medium heat, until bubbly. Keep hot.

For biscuit topper, in medium bowl, combine biscuit mix, 2 tablespoons sugar and cream; mix well. Spoon biscuit batter in 8 mounds over hot berry mixture.

Cover skillet and place on edge of grill over medium-hot **Kingsford® briquets.** Cook, on covered grill, about 15 minutes or until done. Serve warm with vanilla ice cream.

Western Chestnuts and Tenderloin Barbecue:
Roasted Chestnuts, Grilled Tenderloin with Cognac,
Garlic Mushrooms and Fresh Blackberry Cobbler

Pacific Coast Salmon Barbecue

- Grilled Oysters
- Pacific Coast Barbecued Salmon
- Marinated Vegetable Salad with Herbed Salad Dressing
- Grill-Baked Sweet Potatoes
- Sour Cream Biscuits
- Sherbet or Ice Cream

To prepare this menu, you'll need to use 70 Kingsford® Charcoal Briquets (about 4½ pounds).

GRILLED OYSTERS

Makes 4 appetizer servings

12 to 16 fresh oysters in shells
½ cup butter or margarine
2 tablespoons lemon juice
2 tablespoons chopped parsley

Thoroughly scrub oysters. Arrange oysters on grid; do not open shells. Grill oysters, on uncovered grill, over medium-hot **Kingsford® briquets** 12 to 15 minutes or until shells steam open. (Discard any oysters that do not open.)

Meanwhile, in saucepan, combine butter, lemon juice and parsley. Heat butter mixture on edge of grill until butter is melted, stirring frequently.

Carefully remove cooked oysters from grill and serve hot with lemon-butter mixture spooned over.

PACIFIC COAST BARBECUED SALMON

Makes 4 servings

4 fresh or frozen salmon steaks, 1 inch thick
** (about 8 ounces each)**
½ cup butter or margarine
2 tablespoons fresh lemon juice
1 tablespoon Worcestershire sauce

Thaw salmon steaks, if frozen. In saucepan, combine butter, lemon juice and Worcestershire sauce; simmer 5 minutes, stirring frequently. Brush salmon steaks with butter mixture. Place steaks in well-greased wire grill basket.

Grill steaks, on uncovered grill, over medium-hot **Kingsford® briquets** 6 to 9 minutes or until lightly browned. Baste steaks with butter mixture and turn; grill 6 to 9 minutes longer, basting often, until fish flakes easily when tested with fork.

SOUR CREAM BISCUITS

Makes 8 biscuits

1¼ cups all-purpose flour
1½ teaspoons baking powder
½ teaspoon salt
¼ teaspoon baking soda
½ cup sour cream
¼ cup light cream or milk

In bowl, stir together flour, baking powder, salt and baking soda. In small bowl, combine sour cream and light cream. Make a well in center of dry ingredients; add sour cream mixture. Stir just until dough clings together and forms a ball.

Knead dough gently on lightly floured surface 10 to 12 strokes. Roll or pat to ½-inch thickness. Cut dough into 2¼-inch rounds. Using metal spatula, carefully transfer cut biscuits to lightly greased baking sheet. Bake in 375°F oven about 15 minutes or until golden. Serve warm.

Pacific Coast Salmon Barbecue:
Grilled Oysters, Pacific Coast Barbecued Salmon,
Marinated Vegetable Salad (page 24) and
Sour Cream Biscuits

MARINATED VEGETABLE SALAD

Makes 4 servings

6 medium carrots, diagonally sliced into ¼-inch pieces
1 medium zucchini, cut into 2-inch julienne strips
1 medium red onion, thinly sliced and slices halved
¼ cup chopped red or green pepper
1 tablespoon chopped parsley
　Herbed Salad Dressing (recipe follows)

In large saucepan, cook carrots, covered, in boiling salted water to cover for 2 minutes. Add zucchini; return to boil. Cook, covered, 2 minutes longer or until vegetables are just tender. Drain; rinse under cold running water and drain again. Transfer vegetables to bowl. Add onion, red pepper and parsley. Toss with Herbed Salad Dressing. Cover and refrigerate several hours or overnight.

HERBED SALAD DRESSING

Makes ½ cup

¼ cup olive or vegetable oil
¼ cup vinegar
2 tablespoons grated Parmesan cheese (optional)
¼ teaspoon dried oregano, crushed
¼ teaspoon dried basil, crushed
⅛ teaspoon salt

In screw-top jar, combine all ingredients. Cover and shake well.

GRILL-BAKED SWEET POTATOES

Makes 4 servings

4 medium sweet potatoes
　Vegetable oil
4 tablespoons butter or margarine
4 tablespoons brown sugar

Tear off four 6×9-inch pieces of heavy-duty foil. Brush sweet potatoes with oil. Pierce several times with fork. Wrap potatoes in foil. Grill potatoes, on uncovered grill, over medium-hot **Kingsford®** **briquets** about 1 hour or until tender, turning once. Remove foil. Open potatoes with tines of fork and push ends to fluff. Top each with 1 tablespoon butter and 1 tablespoon brown sugar.

Western Rockies Beef Ribs and Pineapple Barbecue

- Jalapeño Pepper Jelly with Cream Cheese and Assorted Crackers
- Barbecued Beef Short Ribs
- Spicy Rice Molds
- Tossed Green Salad
- Flaming Pineapple
- Cabernet Sauvignon Wine

To prepare this menu, you'll need to use about 100 Kingsford® Charcoal Briquets (about 7 pounds).

BARBECUED BEEF SHORT RIBS

Makes 8 servings

6 pounds beef short ribs, cut into 1-rib pieces
1 cup water
¾ cup soy sauce
⅔ cup dry sherry
½ cup packed dark brown sugar
6 cloves garlic, minced
1 tablespoon cayenne pepper
1 tablespoon grated fresh ginger
2 teaspoons Chinese five-spice powder

Trim excess fat from ribs. In large roasting pan, arrange ribs in single layer. For marinade, in medium saucepan, combine remaining ingredients. Cook over medium heat until sugar is dissolved. Remove from heat; cool slightly. Pour marinade over ribs. Cover and refrigerate 1 hour, turning ribs once.

Cover roasting pan with foil. Arrange medium-hot **Kingsford®** **briquets** around drip pan. Place roasting pan on grill; cover grill and cook ribs 45 minutes. Remove ribs from roasting pan and cook, on covered grill, 45 to 60 minutes longer or until ribs are tender, turning and brushing with marinade occasionally. Brush ribs again with marinade just before serving. Bring remaining marinade to boil; reserve ⅓ cup marinade to spoon over Spicy Rice Molds, if desired.

Western Rockies Beef Ribs and Pineapple Barbecue:
Barbecued Beef Short Ribs with Spicy Rice Molds
and Flaming Pineapple (recipes on page 26)

JALAPEÑO PEPPER JELLY

Makes 6 half-pints

1 large green pepper, cut into quarters
2 fresh jalapeño peppers, seeds and ribs removed
6½ cups sugar
1½ cups cider vinegar
½ of 6-ounce package (1 foil pouch) liquid fruit pectin
Several drops green food coloring (optional)

Finely chop green pepper and jalapeño peppers using food processor or knife. In 4½-quart Dutch oven, combine chopped peppers, sugar and vinegar. Bring to boil; reduce heat. Cover and simmer, stirring often, about 15 minutes or until pepper mixture turns transparent.

Stir in pectin; add food coloring. Return to full rolling boil; boil, uncovered, 1 minute, stirring constantly. Remove from heat. Skim off any foam with metal spoon. Pour at once into hot sterilized half-pint jars; seal, using metal lids or paraffin. Serve with cream cheese and assorted crisp crackers, if desired.

SPICY RICE MOLDS

Makes 8 servings

2⅔ cups water
1⅓ cups long grain rice
2 tablespoons butter or margarine
1½ teaspoons soy sauce
3 tablespoons chopped green onion (optional)
3 tablespoons slivered almonds, toasted
2 tablespoons finely chopped parsley

In 2-quart saucepan with tight-fitting lid, combine water, rice, butter and soy sauce. Cover. Bring to boil; reduce heat. Cook 15 minutes; remove from heat. Let stand 10 minutes.

Pack about ½ cup rice mixture into buttered ½-cup mold; unmold onto individual serving plate. Repeat with remaining rice mixture. Sprinkle green onion, toasted almonds and parsley on top of each. Drizzle with ⅓ cup reserved boiled marinade from Barbecued Beef Short Ribs, if desired.

TOSSED GREEN SALAD

Makes 8 servings

2 heads romaine, red leaf or iceberg lettuce
1 cucumber, peeled
4 medium tomatoes, cut into quarters
4 green onions, finely chopped
¼ cup finely chopped fresh basil leaves or parsley
1 cup prepared Hidden Valley Ranch® Original Ranch® Salad Dressing
Salt and pepper

Tear lettuce into bite-size pieces; place in serving bowl and refrigerate, covered with damp paper toweling, to crispen. Slice cucumber in half lengthwise and scoop out seeds. Coarsely chop cucumber. Toss chopped cucumber, tomatoes, onions, basil and lettuce to mix well. Pour dressing on salad and toss to coat. Season to taste with salt and pepper.

FLAMING PINEAPPLE

Makes 8 servings

1 fresh pineapple
½ cup packed light brown sugar
½ teaspoon ground cinnamon
⅛ teaspoon freshly ground nutmeg
¼ cup butter or margarine
½ cup light rum
Ice cream, whipped cream or chilled soft custard (optional)

Cut pineapple in half lengthwise, leaving on green top. Cut each half lengthwise into four sections. Carefully cut pineapple away from peel. Remove core, then cut pineapple into 1-inch chunks; rearrange pineapple chunks on peel. Place in large baking pan or foil pan. Sprinkle with brown sugar, cinnamon and nutmeg; dot with butter. Place pan on edge of grill. Heat pineapple, on covered grill, over medium-hot **Kingsford®** briquets 10 minutes; remove pan from grill.

In small saucepan, heat rum on range-top over low heat just until hot. Carefully ignite with match; pour flaming rum over pineapple, stirring sauce and spooning over pineapple. Serve with ice cream.

Midwest Italian-Style Capon Dinner

- Marinated Artichoke
- Grilled Capon
- Creamy Potato Bake
- Italian-Style Peppers
- Italian Bread with Butter
- Hot Fruit with Pound Cake

To prepare this menu, you'll need to use 94 Kingsford® Charcoal Briquets (about 6 pounds).

MARINATED ARTICHOKE

Makes 4 to 6 appetizer servings

1 large fresh artichoke
    Lemon juice
⅓ cup olive or vegetable oil
3 tablespoons vinegar
1 tablespoon sliced green onion
2 teaspoons chopped parsley
1 clove garlic, minced
1 teaspoon sugar
1 teaspoon lemon juice
¼ teaspoon salt
¼ teaspoon dried thyme, crushed
    Dash cayenne pepper

Trim stem and remove loose outer leaves from artichoke. Cut 1 inch off tops; snip off sharp leaf tips. Brush cut edges with lemon juice. In large saucepan, cook artichoke in boiling water 20 minutes or just until tender and inner leaves can be pulled out easily. Drain and cool slightly. Place artichoke in plastic bag; set bag in bowl.

In screw-top jar, combine oil, vinegar, onion, parsley, garlic, sugar, 1 teaspoon lemon juice, the salt, thyme and cayenne. Cover tightly; shake well. Pour marinade over artichoke in bag. Close bag tightly and refrigerate several hours or overnight. Drain artichoke; place on platter to serve.

ITALIAN-STYLE PEPPERS

Makes 6 servings

4 large red or green peppers
3 tablespoons olive or vegetable oil
1 clove garlic, minced
⅛ teaspoon dried oregano, crushed
    Salt and pepper

Cut peppers into quarters lengthwise; remove seeds and ribs. Grill peppers, skin-side down, on uncovered grill, over medium-hot Kingsford® briquets 6 to 8 minutes or until skins begin to wrinkle and show grill marks. Immediately place under cold running water. Gently pat dry with paper toweling.

Slice peppers into ½-inch-wide strips. Heat oil in foil pan on grill. Add pepper strips, garlic and oregano. Cover pan with foil. Cook, on covered grill, over medium-hot coals 15 minutes or until heated through, stirring once. Season to taste with salt and pepper. Serve immediately.

CREAMY POTATO BAKE

Makes 6 servings

5 medium potatoes, peeled and thinly sliced
1 medium onion, sliced
6 tablespoons butter or margarine
⅓ cup shredded Cheddar cheese
2 tablespoons chopped parsley
1 tablespoon Worcestershire sauce
    Salt and pepper
⅓ cup chicken broth

Place sliced potatoes and onion on 22×18-inch piece of heavy-duty foil. Dot with butter. Sprinkle with cheese, parsley, Worcestershire sauce, salt and pepper. Fold up foil around potatoes; add chicken broth. Seal edges tightly.

Grill packet, on covered grill, over medium-hot Kingsford® briquets about 35 minutes or until potatoes are tender.

GRILLED CAPON

Makes 6 servings

1 capon or whole roasting chicken (6 to 7 pounds)
Salt
¼ teaspoon poultry seasoning
1½ medium onions, quartered
1 tablespoon rubbed sage
2 stalks celery with leaves, cut into 1-inch pieces
2 medium carrots, cut into ½-inch pieces
2 tablespoons butter or margarine, melted
K.C. Masterpiece® Barbecue Sauce

Wash capon thoroughly under cold running water; pat dry with paper toweling. Rub cavity lightly with salt and poultry seasoning. Insert a few onion quarters in neck and fold neck skin over onion. Fold wings across back with tips touching to secure neck skin. Sprinkle 1 teaspoon of the sage in body cavity and stuff with remaining onion quarters, the celery and carrots. Tie legs and tail together with kitchen twine. Insert meat thermometer in center of thigh muscle, not touching bone. Brush skin with melted butter. Rub with remaining 2 teaspoons sage.

Arrange medium-hot **Kingsford® briquets** around drip pan. Place capon, breast-side up, over drip pan; cover grill and cook 1½ to 2 hours or until thermometer registers 185°F. Tent with heavy-duty foil to prevent overbrowning, if necessary. Brush capon with barbecue sauce during last 10 minutes of cooking. Garnish with parsley; serve with additional heated barbecue sauce, if desired.

HOT FRUIT WITH POUND CAKE

Makes 6 servings

2 cans (16 ounces each) fruits for salad
¼ cup Madeira or port wine
2 tablespoons butter or margarine
¾ teaspoon grated fresh ginger
1 pound cake (10¾ ounces), sliced and lightly toasted
Vanilla ice cream (optional)

Drain fruit; reserve ½ cup syrup. Cut up any large pieces of fruit. In heavy skillet or foil pan, combine fruit, reserved syrup, wine, butter and ginger; place skillet on grill. Heat fruit mixture, on covered grill, over medium-hot **Kingsford® briquets** 15 to 20 minutes or until heated through, stirring once. Spoon warm fruit mixture over toasted pound cake slices. Top each serving with vanilla ice cream.

Midwest Italian-Style Capon Dinner:
Grilled Capon with Italian-Style Peppers and Creamy Potato Bake (recipes on page 27)

Gulf Coast Shrimp and Mushroom Barbecue

- Sauteed Mushrooms in Garlic Butter
- Bacon-Wrapped Shrimp with Mexican Fried Rice
- Grilled Zucchini
- Cornbread
- Texas Pecan Pralines

To prepare this menu, you'll need to use 50 Kingsford® Charcoal Briquets (about 3 pounds).

SAUTEED MUSHROOMS IN GARLIC BUTTER

Makes 6 servings

¼ cup butter or margarine
¼ cup white wine vinegar
½ teaspoon garlic powder
¼ teaspoon salt
⅛ teaspoon pepper
6 cups fresh mushrooms (1 pound)
1 small red onion, thinly sliced and separated into rings
Chopped parsley

In heavy 10-inch skillet, melt butter, on uncovered grill, directly over medium-hot **Kingsford® briquets**. Stir in vinegar, garlic powder, salt and pepper; add whole mushrooms and onion rings. Cover skillet; cook 10 minutes. Stir vegetables and cook 10 minutes longer. Sprinkle with parsley before serving.

GRILLED ZUCCHINI

Makes 6 servings

3 medium zucchini
Desired seasonings: basil, oregano, thyme, dill weed, lemon pepper, grated Parmesan cheese, celery salt or garlic salt
2 to 3 tablespoons butter or margarine, softened

Cut zucchini into halves lengthwise. Sprinkle 3 halves with desired seasoning. Spread butter on remaining 3 halves. Place seasoned and buttered halves together; cut crosswise and wrap individual servings in heavy-duty foil. Grill zucchini, on uncovered grill, over medium-hot **Kingsford® briquets** 15 to 20 minutes or until tender, turning often.

BACON-WRAPPED SHRIMP

Makes 6 servings

1 pound fresh or frozen shrimp, shelled and
    deveined
1 small onion, finely chopped
½ cup olive or vegetable oil
½ teaspoon sugar
½ teaspoon cayenne pepper
¼ teaspoon salt
¼ teaspoon dried oregano, crushed
½ teaspoon garlic powder
½ pound bacon
    Mexican Fried Rice (recipe follows)

Thaw shrimp, if frozen. Place shrimp in plastic bag;
set in bowl. For marinade, in small bowl, combine
onion, oil, sugar, cayenne pepper, salt, oregano and
garlic powder. Pour marinade over shrimp; close bag.
Marinate shrimp 3 hours in refrigerator, turning
occasionally.

Cut bacon slices into halves lengthwise, then
crosswise. In large skillet, partially cook bacon. Drain
on paper toweling. Drain shrimp; reserve marinade.
Wrap bacon strips around shrimp and secure with
wooden picks. Place shrimp in wire grill basket or on
12×9-inch piece of heavy-duty foil. (If using foil,
puncture foil in several places.)

Grill shrimp, on uncovered grill, over medium-hot
Kingsford® briquets 6 minutes or until bacon and
shrimp are done, turning basket or individual shrimp
once and basting with marinade. Serve with Mexican
Fried Rice.

MEXICAN FRIED RICE

Makes 6 servings

3 tablespoons vegetable oil
1 cup long grain rice
2 cups water
1 cup chili salsa
½ cup chopped green pepper
1 small onion, chopped
1 clove garlic, minced

In 12-inch skillet, heat oil. Add rice; cook until golden
brown, stirring often. Stir in remaining ingredients.
Bring mixture to boil; reduce heat. Cover; simmer 15
to 20 minutes or until rice is tender. Season to taste;
serve with additional salsa, if desired.

CORNBREAD

Makes 6 to 8 servings

2 cups water
½ cup chopped green onions
1 teaspoon salt
1 teaspoon sugar
1 teaspoon pepper
1 cup yellow cornmeal
1 cup white cornmeal
    Vegetable oil

In medium saucepan, bring water to boil with onions,
salt, sugar and pepper. Turn off heat. Combine
cornmeals and add to water mixture in thin stream,
stirring constantly. Cool to room temperature.

Form cornmeal mixture into 3-inch rounds, ½ inch
thick. Heat 1 inch oil to 350°F in deep-fryer or heavy,
deep skillet. Add cornbread rounds in batches—do
not crowd—and cook until golden brown, about 1
minute per side. Using slotted spoon, transfer to
paper toweling to drain. Serve immediately.

TEXAS PECAN PRALINES

Makes about 45 pralines

1 cup granulated sugar
1 cup packed light brown sugar
1 cup buttermilk
¼ teaspoon salt
3 tablespoons butter or margarine
2 cups pecan halves

Butter sides of heavy 2-quart saucepan; add sugars,
buttermilk and salt. Cook over medium-high heat 6 to
8 minutes until boiling, stirring constantly with
wooden spoon to dissolve sugars. (Avoid splashing
mixture on sides of pan.)

Cook over medium-low heat, stirring occasionally, 16
to 18 minutes or until mixture reaches soft-ball stage,
234°F on a candy thermometer (or until syrup, when
dropped into very cold water, forms a soft ball that
flattens when removed from water). Remove pan
from heat.

Add butter; *do not stir*. Cool, without stirring, about 20
minutes or until 150°F. Stir in pecans. Beat vigorously
with wooden spoon 2 to 3 minutes or until candy
begins to thicken but is still glossy. Drop candy by
teaspoonfuls onto wax-paper-lined baking sheet. (If
candy becomes too stiff, stir in a few drops of hot
water.) Let dry until hard. Store in tightly covered
container.

Gulf Coast Shrimp and Mushroom Barbecue:
*Sauteed Mushrooms in Garlic Butter (page 29) and
Bacon-Wrapped Shrimp with Mexican Fried Rice*

Heartland Pork Chops and Fruit Barbecue

- Barbecued Pork Chops
- Corn-Pepper-Sausage Skillet
- Apple Slaw
- Strawberries 'n' Cream

To prepare this menu, you'll need to use 50 Kingsford® Charcoal Briquets (about 3 pounds).

BARBECUED PORK CHOPS

Makes 6 servings

6 pork loin chops, cut 1 inch thick
½ teaspoon seasoned salt
6 slices orange
6 thin slices onion
6 thin slices lemon
⅓ cup K.C. Masterpiece® Barbecue Sauce

Arrange medium-hot **Kingsford® briquets** to one side of grill with drip pan next to briquets. Sprinkle chops with seasoned salt. Place chops over drip pan; cover grill and cook 40 minutes or until nearly done, turning once after 25 minutes.

Top each chop with slices of orange, onion and lemon and about 1 tablespoon barbecue sauce. Cover grill and cook 5 to 10 minutes longer or until chops are tender and thoroughly cooked.

APPLE SLAW

Makes 6 servings

2 red apples, chopped
1 tablespoon lemon juice
1 small head cabbage, shredded (about 5 cups)
¾ cup prepared Hidden Valley Ranch® Original Ranch® Salad Dressing
Pepper

In bowl, toss chopped apples with lemon juice. Add cabbage and salad dressing; toss to thoroughly coat. Season to taste with pepper. Cover; refrigerate before serving.

Heartland Pork Chops and Fruit Barbecue:
Apple Slaw, Corn-Pepper-Sausage Skillet and Barbecued Pork Chops

CORN-PEPPER-SAUSAGE SKILLET

Makes 6 servings

12 ounces Italian or bulk pork sausage
1 cup chopped green or red pepper
1 cup chopped onion
3 cups fresh whole kernel corn *or* 1 package (16 ounces) frozen whole kernel corn, thawed
½ teaspoon garlic salt
¼ teaspoon pepper
¼ teaspoon chili powder
¼ teaspoon ground cumin
  Halved cherry tomatoes (optional)
  Herbed cream cheese, softened (optional)
  Sprig parsley (optional)

Crumble sausage into heavy 10-inch skillet or heavy foil pan. Add green pepper and onion. Place skillet, on covered grill, over medium-hot **Kingsford® briquets** about 15 minutes or until meat is browned, stirring once or twice. Remove from grill; carefully drain off fat.

Stir in corn, garlic salt, pepper, chili powder and cumin; mix well. Cover skillet with foil. Grill, on covered grill, over medium-hot coals, 10 minutes longer or until heated through. Garnish with tomato halves spread with cream cheese; top with parsley sprig.

STRAWBERRIES 'N' CREAM

Makes 6 servings

2 pints fresh strawberries, hulled and halved (4 cups)
¼ cup honey
2 tablespoons orange-flavored liqueur
1 quart vanilla ice cream

Arrange strawberries on 20×18-inch piece of heavy-duty foil. In small bowl, combine honey and liqueur. Drizzle over strawberries. Fold foil loosely around berries; seal edges tightly.

Grill packet, on covered grill, over medium-hot **Kingsford® briquets** 10 to 12 minutes or until berries are heated through. (If coals have cooled to medium, grill packet 12 to 15 minutes or until hot.) Serve hot over vanilla ice cream.

Southwest Mexican Chicken Barbecue

- Over-the-Coals Spiced Popcorn
- Mexican Chicken with Spicy Bacon
- Charcoal-Grilled Tortillas
- Charcoal-Baked Bananas Flambé
- Mexican Beer or Iced Tea

To prepare this menu, you'll need to use 84 Kingsford® Charcoal Briquets (about 5½ pounds).

MEXICAN CHICKEN WITH SPICY BACON

Makes 4 servings

    2 serrano chili peppers
    2 cloves garlic
      Dash ground cloves
      Dash ground cinnamon
    4 slices bacon, partially cooked
    1 whole roasting chicken (3½ to 4 pounds)

Remove stems from peppers. Slit open; remove seeds and ribs. Finely chop peppers and garlic. Place in small bowl. Stir in cloves and cinnamon. Cut bacon into 1-inch pieces.

Lift skin layer of chicken at neck cavity. Insert hand, lifting skin from meat along breast, thigh and drumstick. Using small metal spatula, spread pepper mixture evenly over meat under skin. Place layer of bacon pieces over pepper mixture. Skewer neck skin to back. Tie legs securely to tail with kitchen twine; twist wing tips under back of chicken. Insert meat thermometer in center of thigh muscle, not touching bone.

Arrange medium-hot Kingsford® briquets around drip pan. Place chicken, breast-side up, over drip pan. Cover grill and cook about 1 hour or until meat thermometer registers 185°F. Garnish with grilled cherry tomatoes and additional serrano chili peppers, if desired.

OVER-THE-COALS SPICED POPCORN

Makes about 8 cups

    ½ cup popcorn or 8 cups popped popcorn
    2 tablespoons butter or margarine
    ½ teaspoon Worcestershire sauce
    ½ teaspoon chili powder
    ½ teaspoon lemon pepper
    ¼ teaspoon garlic powder
    ¼ teaspoon onion powder
    ⅛ teaspoon salt

If desired, pop ½ cup popcorn over coals in long-handled fireplace corn popper. Hold directly over, but not touching, hot Kingsford® briquets; shake vigorously until corn is popped, 3 to 4 minutes.

In saucepan, combine remaining ingredients. Set on edge of grill to melt butter. Toss butter mixture with popped popcorn.

CHARCOAL-BAKED BANANAS FLAMBÉ

Makes 4 servings

    4 ripe medium bananas
    4 tablespoons butter or margarine
    ½ cup packed brown sugar
    ¼ teaspoon ground allspice *or* ½ teaspoon ground cinnamon *or* freshly grated nutmeg
    ¼ cup lime juice
    ¼ cup dark rum

Grill unpeeled bananas, on covered grill, over medium-hot Kingsford® briquets about 8 minutes or until just barely tender and darkened in color. Remove from grill.

In 10-inch oven-proof skillet, combine butter, brown sugar and desired spice. Heat directly over medium-hot coals 2 to 3 minutes or until mixture is bubbly. Stir in lime juice.

Slit bananas lengthwise without removing peel. Arrange bananas in skillet. Grill, on uncovered grill, 6 to 8 minutes or until sauce thickens slightly and bananas are tender, spooning sauce over bananas occasionally. Remove skillet from grill.

In small saucepan, heat rum on range-top over low heat just until hot. Carefully ignite with match and pour flaming rum over bananas in skillet. When flame subsides, serve bananas with sauce spooned over.

Southwest Mexican Chicken Barbecue:
Charcoal-Baked Bananas Flambé and Mexican Chicken with Spicy Bacon

GRILLED CHEESE

Makes 6 servings

1 piece raclette cheese* (12 to 16 ounces)
1 tablespoon olive or vegetable oil
½ teaspoon ground oregano
  Sliced crusty French bread or large crackers

Place cheese in 10-inch iron skillet; brush with oil. Sprinkle oregano on top. Place bread slices around cheese in skillet.

Grill cheese, on covered grill, over medium-hot **Kingsford® briquets** 10 minutes or until cheese is very soft. Remove to table; spread cheese on bread slices.

*Raclette cheese is available at specialty cheese shops. You can try another soft cheese, such as Swiss, but cooking time may vary.

FRESH CORN ON THE GRILL

Makes 6 servings

6 ears corn, with silk and husks intact
  Butter or margarine
  Salt and pepper

Turn back corn husks; do not remove. Remove silks with stiff brush; rinse corn under cold running water. Lay husks back into position. Roast ears, on covered grill, over medium-hot **Kingsford® briquets** about 25 minutes or until tender, turning corn often. Remove husks and serve with butter, salt and pepper, as desired.

Rocky Mountain Grilled Lamb Riblets Dinner:
Grilled Cheese, Fresh Corn on the Grill and Western Lamb Riblets

WESTERN LAMB RIBLETS

Makes 6 servings

5 pounds lamb riblets, cut into serving-size pieces
¾ cup chili sauce
½ cup honey
½ cup beer
¼ cup Worcestershire sauce
¼ cup finely chopped onion
1 clove garlic, minced
½ teaspoon red pepper flakes

Trim excess fat from riblets. In saucepan, combine chili sauce, honey, beer, Worcestershire sauce, onion, garlic and red pepper flakes. Heat mixture to boiling. Reduce heat; simmer, covered, 10 minutes. Remove from heat; cool.

Place riblets in plastic bag; set bag in large bowl. Pour marinade over riblets in bag. Close bag securely and refrigerate about 2 hours, turning bag occasionally to distribute marinade evenly.

Drain riblets; reserve marinade. Arrange medium-hot **Kingsford® briquets** around drip pan. Place riblets over drip pan. Cover grill and cook 45 minutes, turning riblets and brushing with marinade twice. Bring remaining marinade to boil and serve with riblets.

HOMEMADE PEACH ICE CREAM

Makes 3 quarts

1¼ cups sugar
1 envelope unflavored gelatin
  Dash salt
4 cups light cream
1 egg, beaten
2 teaspoons vanilla
3 pounds ripe peaches, peeled and mashed (4½ cups)
¼ teaspoon ground mace *or* ¼ teaspoon almond extract

In large saucepan, combine ¾ cup of the sugar, the gelatin and salt. Stir in 2 cups of the cream. Cook and stir over medium heat until gelatin mixture almost boils and sugar dissolves.

Stir about ½ cup hot gelatin mixture into beaten egg; return to saucepan. Cook and stir 2 minutes longer. Cool. Stir in remaining 2 cups cream and the vanilla.

Stir together mashed peaches, remaining ½ cup sugar and the mace. Add to cooled egg mixture; mix well. Freeze in 4- or 5-quart ice cream freezer according to manufacturer's directions.

BEEF

Nothing brings out the flavor of beef better than a charcoal fire, and here you'll find plenty of savory recipes to fire up your appetite: everything from grilled sirloin steak to burgers and kabobs—even a whole brisket for the grill.

GRILLED STEAK WITH HOT SWEET ONIONS

Makes 4 servings

3 large onions, cut into ¼-inch-thick slices
2 tablespoons honey
½ teaspoon dry mustard
½ teaspoon salt
½ teaspoon paprika
½ teaspoon pepper
4 beef loin T-bone or porterhouse steaks, cut 1 inch thick (8 ounces each)

Arrange sliced onions on large square of heavy-duty foil. In small bowl, combine honey and mustard; drizzle over onions. Sprinkle with salt, paprika and pepper. Fold foil loosely around onions and seal edges tightly. Grill packet, on covered grill, over medium-hot **Kingsford® with Mesquite charcoal briquets** 20 minutes or until onions are tender; turn once. Slash any fat around edge of steaks every 4 inches. About 5 minutes after onions start to grill, place steaks on grill with onion packet. Grill 8 to 10 minutes on each side for medium-rare or to desired doneness. Serve onions on top of each steak.

Grilled Steak with Hot Sweet Onions

38

Stuffed Cheese Burgers

STUFFED CHEESE BURGERS

Makes 6 servings

1½ cups shredded Monterey Jack cheese (about 8 ounces)
　1 can (2¼ ounces) chopped black olives
　⅛ teaspoon hot pepper sauce
1¾ pounds ground beef
　¼ cup finely chopped onion
　1 teaspoon salt
　½ teaspoon pepper
　6 hamburger buns
　　Butter or margarine, melted

In large bowl, combine cheese, olives and hot pepper sauce. Divide mixture evenly and shape into 6 balls. Mix ground beef with onion, salt and pepper; shape into 12 thin patties. Place 1 cheese ball in center of each of 6 patties and top each with a second patty. Seal edges to enclose cheese balls. Lightly oil grid. Grill patties, on covered grill, over medium-hot **Kingsford® briquets** 5 to 6 minutes on each side or until done.

Split buns, brush with butter and place, cut-side down, on grill to heat through. Serve Cheese Burgers on buns.

FLANK STEAK WITH GREEN CHILES

Makes 4 servings

　1 beef flank steak (about 2 pounds)
　5 long green chili peppers,* roasted and peeled, reserving juices
　⅓ cup fresh lime juice (about 2 limes)
　2 cloves garlic, minced
　¼ teaspoon salt

Trim excess fat from steak. Place steak in shallow glass dish. Combine remaining ingredients in food processor or blender. Process until smooth, about 40 seconds. Pour marinade over steak; cover and refrigerate at least 3 hours or overnight. Drain steak; discard marinade. Grill steak, on uncovered grill, over medium-hot **Kingsford® briquets** about 6 minutes on each side for rare or to desired doneness. Carve steak diagonally across grain into thin slices.

*1 can (7 ounces) long green chili peppers can be substituted.

*Recipe courtesy of **California Beef Council***

SPICY BEEF SATAY

Makes 4 servings or 24 appetizer kabobs

1 boneless beef sirloin steak, cut ¾ to 1 inch thick (1 to 1¼ pounds)
¼ cup soy sauce
¼ cup dry sherry
2 tablespoons sesame oil
¼ cup sliced green onion
2 cloves garlic, minced
2 tablespoons brown sugar
1 teaspoon ground ginger
1 teaspoon red pepper flakes
½ cup crunchy peanut butter
¾ cup water

Place steak in freezer 30 minutes to firm; slice into ⅛- to ¼-inch-thick strips. In shallow glass dish, combine soy sauce, sherry, sesame oil, onion, garlic, sugar, ginger and ½ teaspoon of the red pepper flakes. Add beef strips; turn to coat with marinade. Cover and refrigerate 2 to 4 hours.

Soak twenty-four 8-inch bamboo skewers in water 20 minutes. Drain beef; reserve 2 tablespoons marinade. Thread beef strips, accordion-style, on skewers.

Meanwhile, in small saucepan, combine reserved marinade, remaining ½ teaspoon red pepper flakes, the peanut butter and water. Heat over low heat 8 to 10 minutes or until sauce is thick and warm (add more water if necessary). Grill kabobs, on uncovered grill, over medium-hot **Kingsford®** briquets 2 minutes. Turn and cook 2 minutes longer. Serve beef strips with sauce.

Note: Assembled kabobs may be refrigerated, covered, 1 to 2 hours before grilling.

*Recipe courtesy of **National Live Stock & Meat Board***

GRILLED FLANK STEAK SANGRITA

Makes 6 servings

1 beef flank steak (2½ to 3 pounds)
1 teaspoon salt
¼ teaspoon pepper
1 teaspoon dried thyme, crushed
¼ cup orange juice concentrate, thawed and undiluted
3 tablespoons vegetable oil
Fruity Wine Sauce (recipe follows)

Lightly score steak and rub with salt, pepper and thyme. In shallow glass dish, combine orange juice concentrate and oil. Add steak; turn to coat with marinade. Cover and refrigerate at least 30 minutes. Drain meat; reserve marinade. Grill steak, on covered grill, over medium-hot **Kingsford®** briquets 8 to 10 minutes on each side, turning once and basting often with marinade, until done. Cut meat across grain into diagonal slices. Serve with Fruity Wine Sauce.

FRUITY WINE SAUCE

Makes about 2 cups

1½ cups red wine
1 orange, thinly sliced
1 lime, thinly sliced
1 apple, thinly sliced
¾ cup chopped green onion with tops
½ cup butter or margarine
2 tablespoons chopped parsley

In small saucepan, combine red wine, fruit and green onion; bring to boil. Stir in butter and parsley; cook and stir until butter is melted and sauce is hot.

Spicy Beef Satay

CHARCOAL BEEF KABOBS

Makes 4 servings

- ½ **cup vegetable oil**
- ¼ **cup lemon juice**
- ½ **package Hidden Valley Ranch® Original Ranch®**
  Salad Dressing Mix
- 2 **pounds beef top round steak, cut into 1-inch**
  cubes
- 2 **medium green peppers, cut into 1-inch squares**
- 1 **medium onion, cut into wedges**
  Cherry tomatoes

In shallow glass dish, combine oil, lemon juice and dry salad dressing mix. Add beef cubes; turn to coat with marinade. Cover and refrigerate 1 hour or longer. Drain beef cubes; reserve marinade. Thread beef cubes, green peppers and onion alternately on skewers. Grill kabobs, on uncovered grill, over medium-hot **Kingsford®** briquets 15 minutes, brushing often with marinade and turning to brown all sides. Add cherry tomatoes to ends of skewers during last 5 minutes of grilling.

Charcoal Beef Kabobs

BACK RIBS

Makes 4 servings

- 4 **pounds beef back ribs**
  Hoisin Barbecue Sauce (recipe follows) *or*
  Pantry Barbecue Sauce (recipe follows)

Grill ribs, on uncovered grill, over medium-hot **Match light®** charcoal briquets 30 minutes; turn every 10 minutes. Brush ribs generously with either Hoisin Barbecue Sauce or Pantry Barbecue Sauce; cook 10 to 15 minutes or until done.

HOISIN BARBECUE SAUCE

Makes 1 cup

- ½ **cup hoisin sauce**
- 2 **tablespoons white wine**
- 2 **tablespoons vegetable oil**
- 2 **tablespoons grated fresh ginger**
- 2 **cloves garlic, minced**

In small bowl, combine all ingredients; mix well.

PANTRY BARBECUE SAUCE

Makes 1 cup

- ¾ **cup catsup**
- ¼ **cup packed brown sugar**
- 2 **tablespoons soy sauce**
- 1 **tablespoon cider vinegar**
- 1 **clove garlic, minced**
- ¼ **teaspoon ground ginger**
- ¼ **teaspoon hot pepper sauce**

In small bowl, combine all ingredients; mix well.

CALIFORNIA-STYLE STEAK

Makes 4 to 6 servings

- 1 **beef sirloin steak, cut 1 to 1½ inches thick**
  (2 pounds)
- ½ **teaspoon olive or vegetable oil**
- 1 **teaspoon Beau Monde seasoning**
- ½ **teaspoon dried orange peel**
- ½ **teaspoon dried lemon peel**
- 1 **teaspoon pepper**
- 1½ **teaspoons seasoned salt**

Rub both sides of steak with oil. Rub Beau Monde, orange and lemon peels, pepper and seasoned salt thoroughly into both sides of steak. Grill steak, on uncovered grill, over medium-hot **Match light® charcoal briquets** 4 minutes on each side or to desired doneness.

Grilled Porterhouse Steaks with Italian-Style Vegetables

GRILLED PORTERHOUSE STEAKS WITH ITALIAN-STYLE VEGETABLES

Makes 4 servings

2 beef porterhouse steaks, cut 1 to 1½ inches thick (about 2 pounds)
2 cloves garlic, minced
1½ teaspoons dried basil leaves, crushed
½ teaspoon pepper
1 tablespoon olive or vegetable oil
1 large zucchini, cut into 1½-inch pieces
1 small onion, cut into thin wedges
1¼ cups sliced mushrooms
¼ teaspoon salt
6 cherry tomatoes, cut into halves

Season steaks with 1 clove of the garlic, ¾ teaspoon of the basil and the pepper. Grill steaks, on uncovered grill, over medium-hot **Kingsford® briquets,** turning once. Steaks cut 1 inch thick require about 16 minutes for rare, 20 minutes for medium. Steaks cut 1½ inches thick require about 22 minutes for rare, 30 minutes for medium. After turning steaks, heat oil in skillet on grid over coals. Add remaining clove garlic, the zucchini and onion and saute 4 to 5 minutes. Add mushrooms, salt and remaining ¾ teaspoon basil. Cook 2 minutes longer, stirring frequently. Add tomatoes; heat through. Serve vegetables with steaks.

*Recipe courtesy of **National Live Stock & Meat Board***

GIANT BURGER

Makes 8 servings

Giant Bun (recipe follows)
2 pounds lean ground beef
¼ cup catsup
3 tablespoons spicy brown mustard
¼ teaspoon pepper
1 medium onion, thinly sliced and separated into rings
2 ounces Swiss cheese, cut into ½-inch strips
1 large tomato, thinly sliced

Prepare Giant Bun. In large bowl, combine ground beef, catsup, mustard and pepper; mix lightly but thoroughly. Line 9-inch round baking pan with plastic wrap or foil. Shape beef mixture into large patty in pan, pressing lightly but firmly. Remove patty from pan. Lightly oil grid. Cook burger, on covered grill, over medium-hot **Kingsford®** briquets 7 minutes. To turn, slide a flat baking sheet under burger. Hold a flat plate over burger, flip over and carefully slide uncooked side onto grid. Grill, covered, 7 minutes

longer or to desired doneness. Arrange onion rings and cheese on top of burger during last minute of cooking. Remove from grill with flat baking sheet.

Toast cut sides of Giant Bun on grid 1 minute. Place burger on bottom half of bun; arrange tomato slices on top. Cover with top half of Giant Bun. Cut into wedges.

GIANT BUN

1 loaf (1 pound) honey cracked wheat frozen bread dough
2 tablespoons butter or margarine, softened

Thaw bread dough as directed on package. Shape into round flat loaf to fit greased 9-inch round baking pan; let rise in warm place until doubled in volume (approximately 4 to 6 hours). Bake in 350°F oven 30 to 35 minutes. Cool. Slice loaf crosswise in half; spread cut sides with butter.

*Recipe courtesy of **National Live Stock & Meat Board***

Giant Burger

WESTFORK BARBECUE

Makes 20 servings

1 whole beef brisket (10 to 13 pounds)
  Garlic powder
  Pepper
6 cups K.C. Masterpiece® Barbecue Sauce
¼ cup wine vinegar
3 tablespoons vegetable oil
1 tablespoon liquid smoke, optional
  French bread rolls
  Sour cream

Trim excess fat from brisket to ¼ inch. Sprinkle brisket with garlic powder and pepper. In large glass dish, combine 2 cups of the barbecue sauce, the vinegar, oil and liquid smoke. Add brisket; turn to coat with marinade. Cover and refrigerate overnight. Drain meat; reserve marinade. Place brisket over very hot **Kingsford® briquets**. Quickly sear both sides (flare-ups will occur). Add one or two handfuls of soaked hickory chips to briquets, if desired. Cover grill and cook brisket 1½ to 2 hours, adding hickory chips as needed to maintain good smoke. Baste with reserved marinade during last ½ hour of grilling. Remove brisket. Carve across grain into thin slices. To make sandwiches, serve on warmed French rolls with remaining barbecue sauce and sour cream.

ORANGE-FLAVORED GRILLED BEEF

Makes 4 servings

1 orange
3 tablespoons soy sauce
2 tablespoons brown sugar
2 tablespoons cider vinegar
½ teaspoon pepper
½ teaspoon chili powder
1 clove garlic, minced
1 teaspoon grated fresh ginger
2 pounds beef round tip roast, cut into 3-inch
    cubes

Grate peel from orange to equal 1 tablespoon. Squeeze juice from orange into large bowl. Stir in remaining ingredients except beef. Add beef cubes; toss to coat with marinade. Cover and refrigerate 8 hours or overnight. Drain meat cubes; reserve marinade. Grill beef cubes, on covered grill, over medium-hot **Kingsford® briquets** 3 minutes. Turn beef cubes, brush with marinade and cook 5 minutes longer or until done.

Honey-Mustard Beef Ribs

HONEY-MUSTARD BEEF RIBS

Makes 4 servings

1 cup butter or margarine
1 bunch green onions with tops, finely chopped
1 small yellow onion, finely chopped
4 cloves garlic, minced
4 tablespoons prepared mustard
4 tablespoons honey
½ teaspoon liquid smoke, optional
1 teaspoon lemon pepper
1 teaspoon brown sugar
5 pounds beef back ribs

In saucepan, combine butter, green onions, yellow onion and garlic. Cook over low heat 15 minutes or until onions are tender. Remove from heat and add remaining ingredients except ribs. Grill ribs, on covered grill, over medium-hot **Kingsford® briquets** 30 to 35 minutes, brushing ribs generously with mustard-honey mixture, until meat is tender.

TERIYAKI STEAK WITH ONIONS

Makes 5 to 6 servings

    1 beef flank steak (about 1½ pounds)
    ½ cup soy sauce
    ¼ cup dry white wine
    2 tablespoons brown sugar
    1 teaspoon grated fresh ginger
    2 cloves garlic, minced
    1 large sweet onion, sliced
    1 tablespoon butter or margarine

Place steak in large plastic bag; place bag in large bowl. In 1-quart measure, combine soy sauce, wine, brown sugar, ginger and garlic. Pour marinade over steak in bag; turn to coat with marinade. Close bag securely and refrigerate 6 to 8 hours or overnight, turning occasionally. Drain meat; reserve marinade. Grill steak, on uncovered grill, over medium-hot **Kingsford®** briquets 10 to 15 minutes or to desired doneness, turning once.

Meanwhile, in skillet, cook onion in butter until soft. Stir in ½ cup reserved marinade; cook 4 to 5 minutes. Carve steak diagonally across grain into thin slices. Serve with cooked onion slices.

*Recipe courtesy of **National Live Stock & Meat Board***

SUNNY SIRLOIN STEAK

Makes 4 to 5 servings

    ½ cup fresh orange juice
    ¼ cup soy sauce
    2 tablespoons dry sherry
    1 clove garlic, minced
    2 dashes ground cloves
    1 beef sirloin steak, cut 1¼ inches thick (about 2 pounds)

In small bowl, combine orange juice, soy sauce, sherry, garlic and cloves. Place steak in plastic bag; place bag in large bowl. Pour marinade over steak in bag; turn steak to coat. Close bag securely and refrigerate 2 to 4 hours, turning steak at least once. Drain meat; discard marinade. Place steak over medium-hot **Kingsford®** briquets. Cover grill and cook 7 to 8 minutes on each side or to desired doneness.

*Recipe courtesy of **National Live Stock & Meat Board***

TEXAS-STYLE STEAK ON HOT BREAD

Makes 4 to 6 servings

    ½ cup olive or vegetable oil
    ¼ cup lime juice
    ¼ cup red wine vinegar
    1 medium onion, finely chopped
    1 clove garlic, minced
    ¼ teaspoon ground cumin
    1 teaspoon chili powder
    ½ teaspoon salt
    1 beef skirt or flank steak (about 1½ pounds)
    1 round loaf French or sourdough bread
    1 cup salsa
    1 cup guacamole

In shallow glass dish, combine oil, lime juice, vinegar, onion, garlic, cumin, chili powder and salt. With meat mallet, pound steak to ¼-inch thickness. Place steak in marinade; turn to coat. Cover and refrigerate several hours or overnight, turning several times. Drain steak; discard marinade. Grill steak, on covered grill, over medium-hot **Kingsford® with Mesquite charcoal briquets** 4 to 8 minutes on each side, or until done. Cut bread into 1-inch slices and toast on grill. Heat salsa. Carve steak into ¾-inch diagonal strips. Arrange steak on toasted bread. Top with hot salsa and guacamole.

BARBECUED BUTTERFLIED EYE ROUND ROAST

Makes 4 to 6 servings

    1 can (12 ounces) beer
    ¼ cup vegetable oil
    ¼ cup cider vinegar
    1 medium onion, chopped
    2 cloves garlic, minced
    ½ teaspoon pepper
    1 beef eye-of-round roast (about 3 pounds), butterflied
    1 cup K.C. Masterpiece® Barbecue Sauce

In shallow glass dish, combine beer, oil, vinegar, onion, garlic and pepper. Add roast; turn to coat with marinade. Cover and refrigerate overnight, turning occasionally. Drain roast; discard marinade. Grill roast, on covered grill, over medium-hot **Kingsford®** briquets 25 minutes, turning and basting often with barbecue sauce. Season with salt, if desired. Carve roast into thin slices. Heat remaining barbecue sauce and serve with beef slices.

Teriyaki Steak with Onions

T-BONE STEAKS WITH POTATO AND ONION KABOBS

Makes 4 servings

**4 beef loin T-bone steaks, cut 1 to 1½ inches thick
   (about 8 ounces each)
Salt and pepper
Potato and Onion Kabobs (recipe follows)**

Season steaks with salt and pepper to taste. Grill steaks, on uncovered grill, over medium-hot **Kingsford® briquets,** turning occasionally, about 16 minutes for rare, 20 minutes for medium. (Steaks cut 1½ inches thick require 22 minutes for rare, 30 minutes for medium). Serve with Potato and Onion Kabobs.

POTATO AND ONION KABOBS

**2 large all-purpose potatoes (about 1½ pounds)
1 large sweet onion
3 tablespoons butter or margarine, melted
1 teaspoon paprika
½ teaspoon celery salt
¼ teaspoon garlic powder
⅛ teaspoon pepper**

In saucepan, cook unpeeled potatoes in boiling water to cover 20 minutes; drain. When cool enough to handle, cut each potato crosswise into four 1-inch-thick slices. Cut onion crosswise into four 1-inch-thick slices. Alternately thread potato and onion slices on each of four 8-inch skewers. In small bowl, combine remaining ingredients. Brush both sides of potatoes and onions with seasoned butter. Grill kabobs, on uncovered grill, over medium-hot **Kingsford® briquets** 20 minutes, turning after 10 minutes and brushing with seasoned butter occasionally.

*Recipe courtesy of **National Live Stock & Meat Board***

ISLANDER'S BEEF BARBECUE

Makes 4 to 6 servings

**1 boneless beef chuck roast (3 to 3½ pounds)
¾ cup apricot-pineapple jam
2 tablespoons soy sauce
1 teaspoon ground ginger
1 teaspoon grated lemon peel**

Slice roast across grain into ¼-inch-thick slices. In bowl, combine remaining ingredients. Grill beef slices, on uncovered grill, over medium-hot **Kingsford® briquets** 8 to 10 minutes. Turn and baste often with jam mixture.

T-Bone Steaks with Potato and Onion Kabobs

Nutty Burgers

NUTTY BURGERS

Makes 6 servings

- 1½ pounds ground beef
- 1 medium onion, finely chopped
- 1 clove garlic, minced
- 1 cup dry bread crumbs
- ⅓ cup grated Parmesan cheese
- ⅔ cup pine nuts
- ⅓ cup chopped parsley
- 2 eggs
- 1½ teaspoons salt
- 1 teaspoon pepper

In large bowl, combine all ingredients. Shape into 6 thick patties. Grill patties, on covered grill, over medium-hot **Kingsford® briquets** 5 minutes on each side or until done. Serve on French bread and garnish with chopped green onion, if desired.

STEAK KABOBS

Makes 6 servings

- 2 pounds beef top round steak
- 1 bottle (8 ounces) French salad dressing
- 2 tablespoons lemon juice
- 1 can (16 ounces) white whole onions, drained
- 18 cherry tomatoes

Place steak in freezer 30 minutes to firm; slice into ¼-inch-thick strips. Place strips in shallow glass dish. Drizzle with salad dressing and lemon juice. Cover and refrigerate at least 4 hours. Drain beef strips; reserve marinade. Thread beef, onions and tomatoes alternately on 6 skewers. Brush with marinade. Grill kabobs, on uncovered grill, over medium-hot **Match light® charcoal briquets** 7 to 10 minutes, turning and basting often, until beef is cooked to desired doneness.

PEPPER-STUFFED FLANK STEAK

Makes 6 to 8 servings

2 beef flank steaks (about 1 pound each)
1¼ teaspoons garlic powder
¼ teaspoon black pepper
1 green pepper, cut into strips
1 red pepper, cut into strips
1 onion, cut into thin slices
1 can (15 ounces) tomato sauce
½ cup finely chopped onion
¼ cup soy sauce
1 tablespoon sugar
1 teaspoon dry mustard
⅛ teaspoon cayenne pepper
¼ cup vegetable oil

With meat mallet, pound each steak to ¼-inch thickness. Sprinkle steaks with ¼ teaspoon of the garlic powder and the pepper. Arrange green and red pepper strips horizontally on steaks. Cover with onion slices. Starting at narrow end of each steak, roll up jelly-roll fashion; tie with kitchen twine. Set aside. In large jar with screw-top lid, combine remaining ingredients except oil. Shake to blend. Brush outsides of beef rolls with oil. Lightly oil grid. Grill steaks, on covered grill, over hot **Kingsford® briquets** about 30 minutes, turning often, until done. Brush steaks with tomato-soy mixture during last 10 minutes of grilling.

GRILLED STEAK WITH MUSHROOM-WINE SAUCE

Makes 4 servings

4 beef loin T-bone, porterhouse or filet mignon steaks, cut 1 inch thick (8 ounces each)
3 tablespoons butter or margarine
½ pound mushrooms, sliced (about 2 cups)
¼ cup white wine
2 tablespoons minced parsley
½ teaspoon dried tarragon, crushed
1 teaspoon instant beef bouillon granules

Slash any fat around edge of steaks every 4 inches. Lightly oil grid. Grill steaks, on covered grill, over medium-hot **Kingsford® with Mesquite charcoal briquets** 8 to 10 minutes on each side for medium-rare, or to desired doneness. While steak is grilling, heat butter in large skillet until hot. Add mushrooms and saute 1 minute or until tender. Add wine, parsley, tarragon and beef bouillon granules; simmer 4 minutes, stirring often. Serve sauce over steak.

BEEF BRISKET, TEXAS-STYLE

Makes 8 to 10 servings

1 beef brisket (6 to 8 pounds)
¾ cup finely chopped onion
2 teaspoons paprika
½ teaspoon pepper
    Water
1 cup prepared steak sauce
    Special Sauce (recipe follows)

Trim fat covering brisket to ¼ inch. In small bowl, combine onion, paprika and pepper. Rub mixture evenly over surface of brisket. Place brisket, fat-side up, in large foil pan. Cover pan tightly with foil. Place pan in center of grill over low **Kingsford® briquets.** Cover grill and cook 5 hours, turning brisket every 1½ hours. (Remove fat from pan with baster.) Add ½ cup water, as needed, to pan. (Be sure to add briquets as needed to maintain low heat.)

Remove foil from pan. Remove brisket; place on grid directly over coals. Combine pan drippings with steak sauce; reserve 1 cup mixture for Special Sauce. Brush some of remaining mixture over brisket. Cover grill and cook brisket 1 hour longer, brushing occasionally with sauce mixture. Cut brisket into thin slices and serve with Special Sauce.

SPECIAL SAUCE

Makes 2 cups

½ cup finely chopped onion
2 tablespoons butter or margarine
1 cup steak sauce mixture (reserved from recipe above)
1 cup catsup
1 tablespoon brown sugar
¼ teaspoon red pepper flakes

In small saucepan, saute onion in butter until tender. Stir in reserved steak sauce mixture, catsup, brown sugar and red pepper flakes. Simmer 10 minutes.

*Recipe courtesy of **National Live Stock & Meat Board***

Beef Brisket, Texas-Style

POULTRY

A range of recipes for your grill, from an easy-to-serve grilled chicken to a chili-fired bird for extra zip. Also included are great ways to grill Cornish hens, and, of course, a classic barbecued turkey.

DAN D'S CHICKEN BBQ

Makes 4 servings

⅓ cup white Zinfandel wine
⅓ cup olive or vegetable oil
1 tablespoon Dijon-style mustard
1 teaspoon dried rosemary, crushed
1 clove garlic, minced
   Salt and pepper
1 broiler-fryer chicken (2 to 3 pounds), quartered

In shallow glass dish, combine all ingredients except chicken. Add chicken; turn to coat with marinade. Cover and refrigerate several hours or overnight, basting occasionally. Drain chicken; reserve marinade. Grill chicken, on covered grill, over medium-hot **Kingsford® briquets** about 15 minutes on each side or until fork-tender, basting often with marinade.

Dan D's Chicken BBQ

54

GRILLED CHICKEN RIBBONS

Makes 4 servings

¼ cup olive or vegetable oil
2 tablespoons lemon or lime juice
2 cloves garlic, minced
1 teaspoon honey
¾ teaspoon dried thyme, crushed
½ to 1 teaspoon red pepper flakes
    Salt and pepper
4 chicken breast halves, skinned and boned
    (about 6 ounces each)

In small bowl, combine all ingredients except chicken; mix well. Cut chicken lengthwise into strips about 1 inch wide. Thread chicken on 8 skewers; brush generously with sauce mixture. Grill chicken, on covered grill, over hot **Kingsford®** briquets 3 to 4 minutes on each side or until chicken is cooked through, basting with sauce once or twice. Serve with green, red, yellow or orange pepper kabobs, if desired.

SPICY SOY-APPLE CHICKEN

Makes 12 servings

1 cup soy sauce
1 can (6 ounces) frozen apple juice concentrate,
    thawed and undiluted
1½ teaspoons dry mustard
1½ teaspoons ground ginger
¾ teaspoon ground cloves
½ teaspoon garlic powder
3 broiler-fryer chickens (2 to 3 pounds each),
    quartered

In small saucepan, combine soy sauce and apple juice concentrate. In small bowl, combine mustard, ginger, cloves and garlic powder. Add ¼ cup of soy-apple liquid to spice mixture; blend thoroughly. Stir spice mixture into remaining liquid in saucepan and bring to boil over medium heat. Place chicken in large shallow glass dish. Pour marinade over chicken; turn to coat with marinade. Cover and refrigerate at least 8 hours or overnight.

Drain chicken; reserve marinade. Lightly oil grid. Grill chicken, on covered grill, over medium-hot **Kingsford®** briquets 1 to 1½ hours or until fork-tender, turning and brushing with marinade every 15 minutes.

Recipe courtesy of **National Broiler Council**

ORIENTAL GAME HENS

Makes 4 servings

4 Cornish game hens (1 to 1½ pounds each)
    Salt
½ cup peanut or vegetable oil
½ cup soy sauce
2 tablespoons brown sugar
1 tablespoon wine vinegar
½ teaspoon grated fresh ginger
    Dash ground cloves

Remove giblets from hens. Remove fatty portion from neck and tail area of hens. Rinse hens under cold running water. Pat hens dry with paper toweling. Sprinkle cavities with salt. Close neck and body openings with skewers. Tie legs together; tuck wings under back and tie with kitchen twine. Arrange hens in shallow microwaveable dish and cover with vented plastic wrap. Microwave at 50% power 10 minutes. For basting sauce, in small bowl, combine remaining ingredients. Lightly oil grid. Grill hens, on uncovered grill, over medium-hot **Kingsford®** briquets 20 minutes or until thigh moves easily and juices run clear, basting often with sauce.

GLAZED CHICKEN

Makes 4 servings

1 jar (16 ounces) orange marmalade
⅓ cup soy sauce
¼ cup cider vinegar
2 cloves garlic, crushed
1 broiler-fryer chicken (2 to 3 pounds), quartered
    Vegetable oil
    Salt and pepper

In small bowl, combine orange marmalade, soy sauce, vinegar and garlic. Brush both sides of chicken with oil; sprinkle with salt and pepper. Lightly oil grid. Grill chicken, skin-side up, on uncovered grill, over medium-hot **Kingsford®** briquets about 45 minutes or until fork-tender, turning often. Brush chicken with marmalade sauce during last 20 minutes of grilling.

Grilled Chicken Ribbons
served with mixed pepper kabobs

TEXAS-BARBECUED CHICKEN

Makes 4 servings

- ½ cup fresh lemon juice
- ¼ cup vegetable oil
- 1 clove garlic, minced
- 2 teaspoons salt
- 1 teaspoon paprika
- 1 teaspoon pepper
- 1 broiler-fryer chicken (2 to 3 pounds), cut into parts
- 1 tablespoon honey

In small saucepan, combine lemon juice, oil, garlic, salt, paprika and pepper. Heat, stirring constantly, 2 to 3 minutes; cool. Place chicken in shallow glass dish; pour marinade over chicken. Cover and refrigerate at least 1 hour. Drain chicken; reserve marinade. Lightly oil grid. Grill chicken, on covered grill, over medium-hot **Kingsford® with Mesquite charcoal briquets** about 30 minutes, turning every 10 minutes. Stir honey into marinade and brush on chicken. Cook chicken about 20 minutes longer or until fork-tender, turning often and brushing with marinade.

*Recipe courtesy of **National Broiler Council***

Apricot-Stuffed Chicken

APRICOT-STUFFED CHICKEN

Makes 4 servings

- 2 tablespoons butter or margarine, melted
- ¼ cup chopped green onion
- ½ teaspoon ground ginger
- ½ cup stuffing mix
- 2 whole chicken breasts, boned, skin on
- 4 fresh California apricots (about ½ pound), halved and pitted
- ½ cup apricot jam
- 1 tablespoon cider vinegar

In medium bowl, combine butter, onion, ¼ teaspoon of the ginger and the stuffing mix. Place chicken skin-side down and pound with meat mallet to flatten slightly. Spoon half the stuffing mixture in a strip along center of each breast. Place apricot halves on top of stuffing. Roll chicken pieces and tie with kitchen twine to enclose stuffing.

Lightly oil grid. Grill chicken rolls, on uncovered grill, over medium-hot **Kingsford® briquets** 15 minutes, turning once or twice. In small bowl, combine apricot jam, vinegar and remaining ¼ teaspoon ginger. Brush chicken rolls with jam mixture and cook 5 to 10 minutes longer or until chicken is cooked through.

*Recipe courtesy of **California Apricot Advisory Board***

TURKEY FILLETS IN SPICY CILANTRO MARINADE

Makes 4 servings

- 1 cup chopped onion
- 1 large tomato, quartered
- ⅓ cup soy sauce
- ¼ cup chopped green pepper
- 3 tablespoons vegetable oil
- 3 tablespoons lime juice
- 2 tablespoons minced cilantro or parsley
- 2 cloves garlic, minced
- ¾ teaspoon pepper
- 4 turkey breast fillets (about ½ pound each)

Place all ingredients, except turkey, in blender; blend 30 seconds. Place turkey fillets in large plastic bag; place bag in bowl. Pour marinade over turkey in bag. Close bag securely; refrigerate 4 hours, turning occasionally. Drain turkey fillets; reserve marinade. Grill turkey, on uncovered grill, over hot **Kingsford® briquets** 5 minutes on each side or until tender, brushing often with marinade.

GRILLED AND GLAZED GAME HENS

Makes 4 to 6 servings

½ cup K.C. Masterpiece® Barbecue Sauce
¼ cup dry sherry
3 tablespoons frozen orange juice concentrate, thawed and undiluted
4 Cornish game hens (1 to 1½ pounds each)

In saucepan, combine barbecue sauce, sherry and juice concentrate. Bring to boil; simmer 10 minutes. Remove from heat; cool. Remove giblets from hens. Remove fatty portion from neck and tail area of hens. Rinse hens under cold running water. Pat cavities dry with paper toweling; brush with sauce. Grill hens, on covered grill, over medium-hot **Kingsford® briquets** 40 to 50 minutes or until thigh moves easily and juices run clear, turning once. Baste with sauce during last 10 minutes of grilling. Remove from grill; brush generously with additional sauce.

SESAME GRILLED CHICKEN

Makes 4 servings

½ cup white wine
⅓ cup white vinegar
1 tablespoon sesame oil
⅓ cup vegetable oil
2 cloves garlic, sliced
1 tablespoon grated fresh ginger
2 sprigs fresh thyme *or* ¼ teaspoon dried thyme, crushed
1 tablespoon sesame seed
1 broiler-fryer chicken (2 to 3 pounds), quartered

In shallow glass dish, combine all ingredients except chicken. Add chicken; turn to coat with marinade. Cover and refrigerate about 3 hours. Drain chicken; reserve marinade. Grill chicken, skin-side down, on covered grill, over medium-hot **Kingsford® briquets** 15 to 20 minutes, brushing often with marinade. Turn and cook about 20 minutes longer or until fork-tender, brushing often with marinade.

Grilled and Glazed Game Hens

LEMON HERBED CHICKEN

Makes 6 servings

½ cup butter or margarine
½ cup vegetable oil
⅓ cup lemon juice
2 tablespoons finely chopped parsley
2 tablespoons garlic salt
1 teaspoon dried rosemary, crushed
1 teaspoon dried summer savory, crushed
½ teaspoon dried thyme, crushed
¼ teaspoon coarsely cracked black pepper
6 chicken breast quarters with wings attached

In saucepan, combine all ingredients except chicken. Heat until butter melts. Place chicken in shallow glass dish and brush with sauce; let stand 10 to 15 minutes before cooking. Lightly oil grid. Grill chicken, skin-side up, on uncovered grill, over medium-hot **Kingsford® briquets** 30 to 45 minutes or until fork-tender, turning and basting with sauce every 10 minutes.

GRILLED GAME HENS, TEXAS-STYLE

Makes 4 servings

1 can (8 ounces) tomato sauce
¼ cup vegetable oil
1½ teaspoons chili powder
1 teaspoon paprika
¼ teaspoon garlic powder
¼ teaspoon cayenne pepper
4 Cornish game hens (1 to 1½ pounds each), cut into halves

In small bowl, combine all ingredients except game hens. Brush hens generously with tomato mixture. Grill hens, on covered grill, over medium-hot **Kingsford® with Mesquite charcoal briquets** 45 to 50 minutes or until fork-tender, brushing frequently with tomato mixture.

GRILLED STUFFED CHICKEN BREASTS

Makes 6 servings

6 chicken breast halves, skinned and boned
6 tablespoons butter or margarine
3 tablespoons Dijon-style mustard
6 slices cooked ham
1 cup shredded Swiss cheese (about 4 ounces)
3 tablespoons vegetable oil
1 tablespoon honey
Salt and pepper

With meat mallet, pound chicken breasts to ¼-inch thickness. In small bowl, blend butter with 2 tablespoons of the mustard; spread over one side of each chicken breast. Cut ham slices to fit chicken breasts. Place 1 ham slice on each breast; top with shredded cheese. Roll chicken pieces and skewer each to enclose ham and cheese. In small bowl, combine remaining 1 tablespoon mustard, the oil and honey; brush on all sides of each roll. Grill chicken, on covered grill, over medium-hot **Kingsford® briquets** 25 to 35 minutes or until chicken is tender, basting often with mustard-honey mixture.

ZINGY BARBECUED CHICKEN

Makes 4 servings

½ cup grapefruit juice
½ cup apple cider vinegar
½ cup vegetable oil
¼ cup chopped onion
1 egg
½ teaspoon celery salt
½ teaspoon ground ginger
⅛ teaspoon pepper
1 broiler-fryer chicken (2 to 3 pounds), cut into parts

Place all ingredients except chicken in blender or food processor; blend 30 seconds. Pour sauce mixture into small saucepan and heat over low heat about 5 minutes or until slightly thick; remove from heat. Dip chicken in sauce, 1 piece at a time, turning to coat thoroughly. Grill chicken, skin-side up, on covered grill, over medium-hot **Kingsford® briquets** 45 minutes to 1 hour or until fork-tender, turning and brushing with sauce every 15 minutes.

Note: Watch chicken carefully, because egg may cause chicken to become too brown.

Recipe courtesy of **National Broiler Council**

Lemon Herbed Chicken

LEMON-YOGURT GRILLED CHICKEN

Makes 4 servings

1 cup plain yogurt
¼ cup minced fresh parsley
2 tablespoons lemon juice
2 tablespoons vegetable oil
2 tablespoons grated onion
1 tablespoon honey
3 cloves garlic, minced
1 broiler-fryer chicken (2 to 3 pounds), quartered

In small bowl, combine yogurt, parsley, lemon juice, oil, onion, honey and garlic. Place chicken in shallow glass dish. Brush marinade on all sides. Cover and refrigerate at least 3 hours. Drain chicken; reserve marinade. Lightly oil grid. Grill chicken, on covered grill, over medium-hot **Kingsford® briquets** about 45 to 60 minutes or until fork-tender, turning and basting with marinade every 15 minutes.

*Recipe courtesy of **National Broiler Council***

Lemon-Yogurt Grilled Chicken

GRILLED TURKEY WITH VEGETABLE PIZZAZZ

Makes 6 servings

1½ pounds turkey breast, cut into 2-inch pieces
2 medium zucchini, cut into 1-inch chunks
12 large mushrooms
1 medium red pepper, cut into 1½-inch pieces
12 jumbo pimiento-stuffed olives
1 tablespoon vegetable oil
1 cup pizza sauce
1 tablespoon dried basil, crushed

Thread turkey, zucchini, mushrooms, pepper and olives alternately on skewers; brush thoroughly with oil. In small bowl, combine pizza sauce and basil. Grill kabobs, on uncovered grill, over medium-hot **Match light® charcoal briquets** about 10 minutes, turning occasionally. Baste with pizza sauce and cook about 15 minutes longer or until turkey is tender and vegetables are cooked, turning and basting 2 to 3 times.

OIL-AND-VINEGAR GRILLED CHICKEN

Makes 4 servings

¼ cup olive oil
¼ cup wine vinegar
2 teaspoons sugar
1 clove garlic, minced
1 teaspoon dry mustard
1 teaspoon salt
½ teaspoon pepper
½ teaspoon dried tarragon, crushed
¼ teaspoon dried rosemary, crushed
1 broiler-fryer chicken (2 to 3 pounds), cut into parts

In glass jar with tight-fitting lid, combine oil, vinegar, sugar, garlic, mustard, salt, pepper, tarragon and rosemary; cover and shake well to blend. Place chicken in shallow glass dish; pour marinade over. Turn chicken pieces to coat. Cover and refrigerate at least 3 hours or overnight. Drain chicken; reserve marinade. Lightly oil grid. Grill chicken, on covered grill, over medium-hot **Kingsford® briquets** 45 to 60 minutes* or until fork-tender, turning often and brushing with marinade.

*To shorten grilling time, you can precook the chicken in a microwave oven. Place drained chicken in microwave-safe dish, cover loosely and microwave at 100% power 18 minutes, turning every 6 minutes. Grill over medium-hot coals about 12 to 15 minutes or until fork-tender, brushing with marinade.

*Recipe courtesy of **National Broiler Council***

Chicken Fajitas

CHICKEN FAJITAS

Makes 6 servings

½ cup vegetable oil
⅓ cup lime juice
¼ cup red wine vinegar
¼ cup finely chopped onion
2 cloves garlic, minced
1 teaspoon sugar
1 teaspoon dried oregano, crushed
½ teaspoon salt
½ teaspoon pepper
¼ teaspoon ground cumin
6 chicken breast halves, skinned and boned
  Flour tortillas
  Chopped tomatoes
  Chopped onion
  Sliced avocado
  Salsa

In shallow glass dish, combine first 10 ingredients; mix well. Add chicken breasts; turn to coat with marinade. Cover and refrigerate 4 hours, turning occasionally. Drain chicken; reserve marinade. Grill chicken, on covered grill, over medium-hot **Kingsford® briquets** 8 minutes; turn and cook 5 to 7 minutes longer or until cooked through, basting often with marinade.

While chicken is grilling, wrap tortillas in large piece of heavy-duty foil and place on edge of grill. Heat about 10 minutes, turning packet once. Slice chicken breasts into thin slices. Place slices of chicken and garnishes in warm flour tortillas and roll up.

*Recipe courtesy of **Weber Grills***

BARBECUED TURKEY WITH HERBS

Makes 8 to 10 servings

1 turkey (9 to 13 pounds), fresh or frozen, thawed
¾ cup vegetable oil
½ cup chopped fresh parsley
2 tablespoons chopped fresh sage *or*
    2 teaspoons dried sage, crushed
2 tablespoons chopped fresh rosemary *or*
    2 teaspoons dried rosemary, crushed
1 tablespoon chopped fresh thyme *or* 1 teaspoon
    dried thyme, crushed
Salt and coarsely cracked black pepper

Remove neck and giblets from turkey. Rinse turkey under cold running water; drain and pat dry with paper toweling. In small bowl, combine remaining ingredients. Brush cavities and outer surface of turkey generously with herb mixture. Pull skin over neck and secure with skewer. Fold wings behind back and tie legs and tail together with kitchen twine. Insert meat thermometer into center of thickest part of thigh, not touching bone.

Arrange medium-hot **Kingsford® briquets** around large drip pan. Position turkey directly over drip pan. Cover grill and cook turkey 11 to 13 minutes per pound or until internal temperature reaches 185°F, basting occasionally with herb mixture. Add more briquets as necessary, following guidelines for indirect cooking (page 4) for number of briquets needed. Garnish with additional fresh herbs, if desired.

CHICKEN KYOTO

Makes 4 servings

1 cup apple cider
½ cup soy sauce
½ cup vegetable oil
¼ cup sugar
2 teaspoons ground ginger
1 broiler-fryer chicken (2 to 3 pounds), quartered

In small saucepan, combine all ingredients except chicken. Simmer over medium heat 5 to 8 minutes or until sugar is dissolved. Place chicken in shallow glass dish. Pour marinade over chicken; cover and refrigerate about 6 hours. Drain chicken; reserve marinade. Grill chicken, on uncovered grill, over medium-hot **Kingsford® briquets,** about 25 minutes on each side or until fork-tender, basting often with marinade.

SUPER SIMPLE SURPRISE CHICKEN

Makes 4 servings

¼ butter or margarine
3 tablespoons lemon juice
1 teaspoon crab boil (seafood spice blend)
1 teaspoon garlic salt
1 broiler-fryer chicken (2 to 3 pounds), quartered
Lemon wedges

In saucepan, melt butter. Stir in lemon juice, crab boil and garlic salt. Place chicken in shallow glass dish. Pour marinade over chicken; turn to coat with marinade. Cover and refrigerate at least 3 hours or overnight. Drain chicken; reserve marinade. Lightly oil grid. Grill chicken, on covered grill, over medium-hot **Kingsford® briquets** about 1 hour or until fork-tender, turning and brushing with marinade every 15 minutes. Serve with lemon wedges.

*Recipe courtesy of **National Broiler Council***

BARBECUED CHICKEN

Makes 4 servings

1 cup chicken broth
¼ cup catsup
2 tablespoons vinegar
2 tablespoons Worcestershire sauce
2 tablespoons finely chopped onion
1 teaspoon dry mustard
½ teaspoon garlic salt
½ teaspoon salt
¼ teaspoon pepper
1 broiler-fryer chicken (2 to 3 pounds), quartered

In small saucepan, combine all ingredients except chicken. Bring to boil; cool slightly. Place chicken in shallow glass dish. Pour warm sauce over chicken; cover and refrigerate at least 2 hours. Grill chicken, skin-side up, on uncovered grill, over medium-hot **Kingsford® briquets** 45 to 60 minutes or until chicken is fork-tender, turning frequently and basting with marinade.

Barbecued Turkey with Herbs

TASTY GRILLED CHICKEN

Makes 4 servings

¼ teaspoon pepper
4 broiler-fryer chicken leg-thigh quarters
1 can (10½ ounces) beef broth
3 tablespoons soy sauce
1 lemon, thinly sliced
1 tablespoon olive or vegetable oil
1 tablespoon red wine vinegar
1 tablespoon white wine
1 clove garlic, minced

Rub pepper into chicken quarters. In shallow glass dish, combine beef broth, soy sauce, lemon, oil, vinegar, wine and garlic. Add chicken; turn to coat with marinade. Cover and refrigerate at least 3 hours or overnight. Drain chicken; reserve marinade. Lightly oil grid. Grill chicken, on covered grill, over medium-hot **Kingsford®** briquets about 1 hour or until fork-tender, turning and brushing with marinade every 10 minutes.

*Recipe courtesy of **National Broiler Council***

Kansas City–Style Barbecued Chicken Legs

KANSAS CITY–STYLE BARBECUED CHICKEN LEGS

Makes 6 servings

½ cup butter or margarine, softened
⅓ cup finely chopped parsley
2 cloves garlic, minced
2¾ to 3 pounds chicken legs (about 12 legs)
3 tablespoons olive or vegetable oil
¾ cup K.C. Masterpiece® Barbecue Sauce

In small bowl, blend butter, parsley and garlic. Rinse chicken legs under cold running water; pat dry with paper toweling. Starting at thick end of each leg, work finger between skin and meat to form a pocket. Insert about 2 teaspoons parsley butter into pocket; massage outer skin to spread filling. Rub completed legs with oil. Lightly oil grid. Grill chicken, on covered grill, over medium-hot **Kingsford®** briquets about 45 minutes or until fork-tender. Turn and baste occasionally with remaining oil. Baste thoroughly with barbecue sauce during last 15 minutes of grilling. Baste once more before serving. Serve with additional warmed barbecue sauce, if desired.

BARBECUED TURKEY DRUMSTICKS

Makes 4 to 6 servings

1 medium onion, finely chopped
½ cup celery, finely chopped
1 tablespoon butter or margarine
2 tablespoons brown sugar
1 can (8 ounces) seasoned tomato sauce
½ cup catsup
2 tablespoons prepared mustard
1 tablespoon Worcestershire sauce
1 cup water
4 to 6 turkey drumsticks

In saucepan, saute onion and celery in butter until onion is soft and translucent. Stir in remaining ingredients except drumsticks. Lightly oil grid. Grill drumsticks, on covered grill, over medium-hot **Kingsford®** briquets 1 to 1½ hours, turning occasionally. Baste with sauce during last 15 minutes of grilling. Bring remaining sauce to boil and serve with drumsticks.

*Recipe courtesy of **National Turkey Federation***

CHILI-TOMATO GRILLED CHICKEN

Makes 6 to 8 servings

½ cup finely chopped onion
1 clove garlic, minced
2 tablespoons vegetable oil
1 chicken bouillon cube
½ cup hot water
1 can (8 ounces) taco sauce or tomato sauce
2 tablespoons vinegar
1 tablespoon prepared mustard
1 teaspoon salt
¼ teaspoon dried oregano, crushed
2 broiler-fryer chickens (2 to 3 pounds), quartered
1 tablespoon mild chili powder

In small skillet, saute onion and garlic in oil about 3 minutes or until onion is soft and translucent. Dissolve bouillon cube in hot water. Add bouillon, taco sauce, vinegar, mustard, salt and oregano to skillet. Dip chicken in sauce, turning to coat thoroughly; lightly sprinkle on all sides with chili powder. Refrigerate chicken until ready to grill. Add remaining chili powder to sauce; bring to boil and remove from heat; cool slightly.

Just before grilling, redip each chicken piece in sauce. Lightly oil grid. Grill chicken, on covered grill, over medium-hot **Kingsford® briquets** 25 to 30 minutes, turning often. Brush chicken with sauce and cook 20 to 30 minutes longer or until fork-tender, turning and brushing with sauce every 10 minutes.

*Recipe courtesy **National Broiler Council***

APPLE-STUFFED CHICKEN

Makes 6 servings

1 large roasting chicken (5 to 6 pounds)
　Salt-free seasoning and seasoned pepper
2 Granny Smith apples, cored and quartered
3 large leeks, trimmed, washed and cut into
　2-inch pieces
4 or 5 sprigs fresh tarragon, rosemary *or* parsley
⅓ cup butter or margarine, melted
1 tablespoon Kitchen Bouquet® browning sauce

Remove giblets and neck from chicken. Rinse chicken under cold running water; pat dry with paper toweling. Season inside with salt-free seasoning and pepper. Place apples, leeks and herbs in chicken cavity. Pull skin over neck and body openings; secure with skewers. Fold wing tips under body; secure with kitchen twine wrapped around wings and body. Bring legs together and tie at tip ends.

In small bowl, combine butter and browning sauce; brush on chicken. Grill chicken, breast-side down, on covered grill, over medium-hot **Kingsford® with Mesquite charcoal briquets** 25 minutes, basting once with butter sauce. Turn chicken breast-side up and baste again. Cover grill and cook 15 minutes longer; baste again with butter sauce. Cook 35 minutes longer or until thigh moves easily and juices run clear, adding briquets as necessary to maintain heat.

Chili-Tomato Grilled Chicken

PORK & LAMB

Pork has long been one of America's favorites for barbecue, and the hearty flavor of lamb makes it a natural for outdoor cooking. Enjoy simple chops, spicy ribs, exotic kabobs or a variety of whole roasts.

TERIYAKI PORK CHOPS

Makes 4 servings

¼ cup soy sauce
¼ cup peanut or vegetable oil
¼ cup minced onion
3 tablespoons honey
3 tablespoons dry sherry
2 teaspoons grated fresh ginger *or* ¾ teaspoon
   ground ginger
1 clove garlic, minced
4 pork loin chops, cut 1 inch thick

In shallow glass dish, combine all ingredients except pork chops. Add pork chops; turn to coat with marinade. Cover and refrigerate several hours or overnight, basting occasionally. Drain chops; reserve marinade. Arrange medium-hot **Kingsford® briquets** to one side of grill with drip pan next to briquets. Place chops over drip pan. Cover grill and cook 30 to 40 minutes or until chops are tender and cooked through, turning once and basting often with marinade.

Teriyaki Pork Chops

ITALIANO FRANKABOBS

Makes 4 servings

½ cup vegetable oil
2 teaspoons dried oregano, crushed
½ teaspoon ground nutmeg
⅛ teaspoon dried thyme, crushed
⅛ teaspoon dried marjoram, crushed
1 clove garlic, cut in half
8 medium fresh mushrooms
1 medium green pepper, cut into 1-inch pieces
2 large tomatoes, cut into wedges
1 medium zucchini, peeled and cut into 12 slices
2 pounds hot dogs, cut into bite-size pieces

In large bowl, combine oil, oregano, nutmeg, thyme, marjoram and garlic. Add mushrooms, pepper, tomatoes and zucchini. Cover and refrigerate 1 hour or overnight. Alternately thread vegetables and hot dog pieces on 4 skewers. Grill kabobs, on uncovered grill, over medium-hot **Kingsford®** **briquets** about 10 minutes or just until hot dogs are heated through and vegetables tender-crisp, turning often and brushing with marinade.

*Recipe courtesy of **National Hot Dog & Sausage Council***

Italiano Frankabobs

HERBED LAMB AND VEGETABLE KABOBS

Makes 6 servings

½ cup olive or vegetable oil
¼ cup fresh lemon juice
1 tablespoon finely chopped onion
2 teaspoons fresh thyme
1 garlic clove, crushed
1 teaspoon salt
½ teaspoon paprika
1½ pounds boneless lamb, cut into 1½-inch pieces
12 cauliflowerettes
12 slices carrot (1 inch each)
12 small white onions
12 slices zucchini (1 inch each)
12 large fresh mushrooms

In large bowl, combine oil, lemon juice, chopped onion, thyme, garlic, salt and paprika. Add lamb pieces; turn to coat with marinade. Cover and refrigerate 6 to 8 hours or overnight, turning occasionally. In saucepan, cook cauliflowerettes, carrot and white onions in boiling water to cover until tender-crisp. Thread lamb and all vegetables alternately on skewers. Grill kabobs, on uncovered grill, over medium-hot **Kingsford®** **briquets** 13 to 16 minutes, turning often and basting with marinade.

SPICY COUNTRY RIBS

Makes 6 servings

1 medium onion, finely chopped
3 cloves garlic, crushed
2 tablespoons vegetable oil
1 can (15 ounces) tomato sauce
½ cup red wine
¼ cup packed brown sugar
¾ teaspoon salt
½ teaspoon dry mustard
½ teaspoon chili powder
½ teaspoon hot pepper sauce
⅛ teaspoon pepper
5 pounds country-style spareribs

In medium skillet, saute onion and garlic in oil until onion is soft but not brown. Stir in remaining ingredients except spareribs. Bring to boil; reduce heat and simmer, covered, 20 minutes. Trim any excess fat from ribs. Arrange ribs in shallow glass dish. Cover with plastic wrap, vented. Microwave at 50% power 20 minutes, rearranging ribs once. Remove from oven. Brush ribs with sauce. Lightly oil grid. Grill ribs, on covered grill, over medium-hot **Kingsford®** **briquets** 30 minutes or until cooked through, turning often and basting with sauce.

Butterflied Southern Citrus Barbecue

BUTTERFLIED SOUTHERN CITRUS BARBECUE

Makes 8 servings

1 boneless leg of lamb (6 to 8 pounds), butterflied
1½ cups grapefruit juice
3 tablespoons brown sugar
1 tablespoon grated grapefruit or lemon peel
1 teaspoon ground cloves
2 cloves garlic, minced
½ teaspoon salt
¼ teaspoon pepper
   Few drops hot pepper sauce

Place lamb in large glass or enamel bowl. In small bowl, combine remaining ingredients; pour over lamb. Cover and refrigerate several hours or overnight. Drain lamb; reserve marinade. Grill lamb, on covered grill, over medium-hot **Kingsford® briquets** 1 hour and 15 minutes, adding more briquets as necessary, until meat thermometer registers 140°F for rare, 150°–155°F for medium or 160°F for well-done. Turn lamb once halfway through cooking time. Baste often with marinade.

*Recipe courtesy of **American Lamb Council, Inc.***

SATAY PORK

Makes 4 to 6 servings

½ cup peanut or vegetable oil
¼ cup soy sauce
2 tablespoons chopped peanuts
1 tablespoon Worcestershire sauce
1 tablespoon chopped onion
2 cloves garlic, crushed
2 teaspoons brown sugar
¼ teaspoon curry powder
⅛ teaspoon coriander
3 pounds boneless pork, cut into ½-inch cubes

In shallow glass dish, combine all ingredients except pork. Add pork, turning to coat with marinade. Cover and refrigerate 1 to 2 hours, stirring occasionally. Drain pork; reserve marinade. Thread pork on skewers. Grill kabobs, on uncovered grill, over hot **Kingsford® briquets** 5 to 6 minutes or until cooked through, turning often and basting with marinade.

Sweet & Sour Pork Loin

SWEET & SOUR PORK LOIN

Makes 4 servings

½ cup chicken broth or water
½ cup catsup
2 tablespoons brown sugar
2 tablespoons cider vinegar
2 tablespoons Worcestershire sauce
1 clove garlic, crushed
½ teaspoon salt
¼ teaspoon black pepper
⅛ teaspoon cayenne pepper
1 boneless pork loin roast (2 pounds), tied

In saucepan, combine all ingredients except roast. Heat to boiling. Cut roast crosswise into 4 pieces; arrange in shallow glass dish. Pour sweet and sour mixture over pork. Cover and refrigerate overnight. Drain pork; reserve sweet and sour mixture. Grill pork, on uncovered grill, over medium-hot **Match light® charcoal briquets** 20 to 25 minutes or until pork is cooked through, turning 3 to 4 times and basting often with sweet and sour mixture.

BASQUE LAMB

Makes 4 to 6 servings

¾ cup fresh lemon juice
1 cup dry sherry
½ cup olive or vegetable oil
1 clove garlic, crushed
1 boneless lamb shoulder (3 pounds), left untied
1 bunch chives, chopped
1 clove garlic, chopped
1 bunch parsley, chopped
Salt and pepper

In small bowl, combine lemon juice, sherry, oil and crushed garlic. Let stand 1 hour. Sprinkle inside of roast with an even layer of chives, chopped garlic and parsley. Season with salt and pepper to taste. Roll up meat and tie securely with kitchen twine. Arrange medium-hot **Kingsford® briquets** around drip pan. Fill pan with water. Add hickory chips to coals, if desired. Place roast over drip pan. Cover grill and cook 45 to 60 minutes or until medium-rare, basting often with lemon juice mixture. Remove roast from grill; let stand 15 minutes. Carve into 1-inch-thick slices.

ISLAND LAMB TERIYAKI STICKS

Makes 4 to 6 servings

1 cup soy sauce
½ cup brown sugar
¼ cup vegetable oil
¼ cup vinegar
3 cloves garlic, minced
2 teaspoons sesame seed
2 teaspoons ground ginger
1 teaspoon salt
2 pounds boneless lamb, cut into 1-inch-wide
   strips
   Water chestnuts
   Pineapple chunks
   Cherry tomatoes

In shallow glass dish, combine soy sauce, brown sugar, oil, vinegar, garlic, sesame seed, ginger and salt. Add lamb strips, turning to coat with marinade. Cover and refrigerate several hours or overnight, turning occasionally.

Drain meat; reserve marinade. Alternately thread lamb strips (accordion-style), water chestnuts, pineapple and tomatoes on skewers. Grill, on uncovered grill, over medium-hot **Kingsford®** **briquets** 5 to 6 minutes or to desired doneness, turning kabobs often and brushing with marinade. Serve with hot cooked rice, if desired.

*Recipe courtesy of **American Lamb Council, Inc.***

MEXICAN PORK STRIPS

Makes 4 servings or 16 appetizer kabobs

1 boneless pork loin roast (about 1¼ pounds)
2 tablespoons fresh lime juice
2 tablespoons vegetable oil
2 cloves garlic, minced
1 tomato, seeded and finely chopped
1 avocado, peeled and finely chopped
3 tablespoons chopped green chili peppers
2 tablespoons chopped cilantro or parsley
1 green onion, thinly sliced
¾ teaspoon ground cumin
½ teaspoon salt

Place roast in freezer 30 minutes to firm; slice across grain into ⅛- to ¼-inch slices. Cut each slice in half lengthwise. In small bowl, combine lime juice, oil and garlic. Place pork in plastic bag; place bag in bowl. Pour marinade over pork in bag. Close bag securely and refrigerate 30 minutes, turning occasionally.

For salsa, in medium bowl, combine tomato, avocado, chili peppers, cilantro, onion, cumin and salt; cover and refrigerate until ready to serve.

Drain pork; discard marinade. Thread strips of pork accordion-style on skewers. Grill kabobs, on covered grill, over medium-hot **Kingsford®** **briquets** 6 minutes or until pork is cooked through, turning several times. Serve salsa with kabobs.

*Recipe courtesy of **National Live Stock & Meat Board***

Island Lamb Teriyaki Sticks

Lamb Satay

GRILLED SAUSAGE WITH APPLES & ONIONS

Makes 4 servings

1 pound smoked sausage, cut into 1-inch chunks
2 small apples, cored and cut into quarters
2 small onions, cut into quarters
2 tablespoons apple jelly
1 tablespoon butter or margarine

Thread sausage, apples and onions alternately on 4 skewers. In small saucepan, combine jelly and butter; heat until melted. Brush jelly mixture on sausage kabobs. Grill kabobs, on uncovered grill, over medium-hot **Match light® charcoal briquets** 10 to 15 minutes or until cooked through, turning often and basting with jelly mixture.

RASPBERRY-GLAZED LAMB RIBS

Makes 2 servings

2 lamb ribs, about 6 ounces each (8 ribs per slab)
½ teaspoon salt
¼ teaspoon pepper
¼ teaspoon paprika
½ cup red wine vinegar or raspberry vinegar
½ cup white wine
½ cup seedless raspberry jam
1 tablespoon finely chopped shallots
1 tablespoon cornstarch
1 tablespoon water

Sprinkle ribs with salt, pepper and paprika. In medium saucepan, combine vinegar, white wine, raspberry jam and shallots. Stir over medium heat until jam is melted. Stir together cornstarch and water; add to raspberry mixture and stir until sauce is smooth and clear.

Arrange medium-hot **Kingsford® briquets** around drip pan. Place ribs over drip pan. Cover grill and cook 50 to 60 minutes or until ribs are cooked through, turning ribs every 10 minutes. Brush ribs with sauce during last 10 minutes of grilling.

*Recipe courtesy of **American Lamb Council, Inc.***

LAMB SATAY

Makes 4 servings

1¼ pounds boneless leg of lamb, well trimmed
½ cup lime juice
1 can (20 ounces) pineapple chunks in juice
5 tablespoons creamy peanut butter
Hot cooked rice

Cut lamb into 3×¾×½-inch strips. Place strips in shallow glass dish; add lime juice and toss to coat. Cover and refrigerate at least 1 hour or overnight. Drain lamb strips and pat dry. Thread strips, accordion-style, on 6-inch skewers.

Drain pineapple; reserve juice. Place peanut butter in small saucepan; gradually stir in reserved juice. Cook and stir over medium heat 5 to 6 minutes or until thoroughly heated. Grill lamb strips, on uncovered grill, over medium-hot **Kingsford® briquets** 6 to 7 minutes or to desired doneness, turning often. Serve with peanut sauce, pineapple chunks and hot cooked rice. Garnish with lime slices, if desired.

*Recipe courtesy of **American Lamb Council, Inc.***

Raspberry-Glazed Lamb Ribs

Spicy Lamb Burgers

ALL-AMERICAN PORK RIBS

Makes 4 servings

1 small onion, coarsely chopped
2 tablespoons water
⅔ cup catsup
⅔ cup chili sauce
2 tablespoons lemon juice
½ teaspoon dry mustard
¼ teaspoon cayenne pepper
¼ teaspoon paprika
¼ teaspoon Worcestershire sauce
½ teaspoon salt
3 pounds pork back ribs

For barbecue sauce, in medium saucepan, cook onion in water 3 to 4 minutes. Add catsup, chili sauce, lemon juice, mustard, cayenne, paprika and Worcestershire sauce. Cook over low heat 15 minutes. Sprinkle salt over surface of ribs. Grill ribs, on covered grill, over medium to low **Kingsford® briquets** 45 to 60 minutes or until done, turning occasionally. Brush both sides of ribs with sauce during last 10 minutes of cooking. Bring remaining sauce to boil and serve with ribs.

Note: Recipe can be doubled.

*Recipe courtesy of **National Live Stock & Meat Board***

SPICY LAMB BURGERS

Makes 6 servings

¼ cup chopped onion
1 teaspoon curry powder
1 tablespoon butter or margarine, melted
¼ cup finely chopped almonds
¼ cup crushed pineapple, drained
1½ pounds ground lamb
½ cup dry bread crumbs
2 eggs
⅛ teaspoon pepper
6 pita breads

In skillet, saute onion and curry powder in butter until onion is tender. Stir in almonds and pineapple. In bowl, combine onion mixture thoroughly with lamb, bread crumbs, eggs and pepper. Shape meat mixture into 6 patties. Grill patties, on uncovered grill, over medium-hot **Match light® charcoal briquets** about 5 minutes on each side or until done. Grill pita breads on edge of grill. Serve lamb burgers in pita breads with bean sprouts and plain yogurt, if desired.

GRILLED HERBED ITALIAN SAUSAGE

Makes 6 servings

2¼ pounds fresh mild Italian sausage, cut into 6 pieces
¾ cup dry white wine
¾ teaspoon dried rosemary, crushed
¾ teaspoon dried thyme, crushed
6 kaiser rolls, split
Assorted mustards

Form each piece of sausage into a coil. Secure by inserting skewer horizontally through open end of sausage. Place sausages in shallow glass dish; add wine and herbs, turning sausages to coat with marinade. Cover and refrigerate 2 to 3 hours. Drain sausages; reserve marinade. Grill sausages, on uncovered grill, over low **Kingsford® briquets** 20 to 25 minutes or until cooked through, basting often with marinade. Serve sausages on rolls with assorted mustards.

*Recipe courtesy of **National Live Stock & Meat Board***

GRILLED SMOKED SAUSAGE

Makes 6 servings

1 cup apricot or pineapple preserves
1 tablespoon lemon juice
1½ pounds smoked sausage

In small saucepan, heat preserves. Strain; reserve fruit pieces. Combine strained preserve liquid with lemon juice. Grill whole sausage, on uncovered grill, over low **Kingsford® briquets** 5 minutes. Brush with glaze; grill sausage about 5 minutes longer, turning and brushing with glaze occasionally. Garnish with fruit pieces.

GRILLED HAM SANDWICHES

Makes 6 servings

1 pound boneless fully cooked ham, in 1 piece
1 cup catsup
⅓ cup butter or margarine
1½ tablespoons Worcestershire sauce
1½ tablespoons prepared mustard
1 teaspoon onion salt
6 buttered hot dog buns

Cut ham lengthwise into 6 slices. In small saucepan, combine catsup, butter, Worcestershire sauce, mustard and onion salt. Cook over low heat until mixture simmers. Remove sauce from heat; cool slightly.

Coat ham slices with sauce. Grill ham slices, on uncovered grill, over medium-hot **Match light® charcoal briquets** 3 to 4 minutes on each side or until meat is browned and hot. Serve sliced ham in hot dog buns.

CIDER-GLAZED PORK ROAST

Makes 6 servings

½ cup apple cider
¼ cup Dijon-style mustard
¼ cup vegetable oil
¼ cup soy sauce
1 boneless pork loin roast (4 to 5 pounds), tied

In small bowl, combine apple cider, mustard, oil and soy sauce. Insert meat thermometer in center of thickest part of roast. Arrange medium-hot **Kingsford® briquets** around drip pan. Place roast over drip pan. Cover grill and cook 2½ to 3 hours or until meat thermometer registers 170°F, adding more briquets as necessary. Brush roast with cider mixture 3 or 4 times during last 30 minutes of cooking.

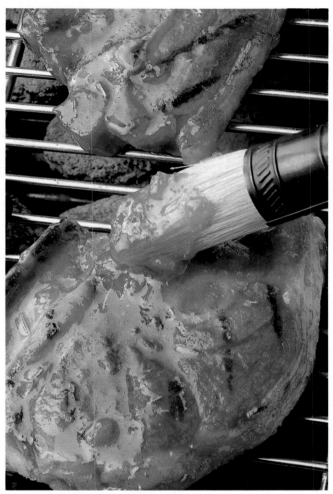

Apricot-Glazed Lamb Chops

APRICOT-GLAZED LAMB CHOPS

Makes 4 servings

⅓ cup apricot jam
1 tablespoon white vinegar
1 teaspoon Dijon-style mustard
½ teaspoon dried rosemary, crushed
1 clove garlic, minced
½ teaspoon salt
¼ teaspoon pepper
4 lamb shoulder arm or blade chops, cut ¾ inch thick

In small saucepan, combine apricot jam, vinegar, mustard, rosemary, garlic, salt and pepper. Cook over low heat, stirring, until jam is melted. Grill lamb chops, on uncovered grill, over medium-hot **Kingsford® briquets** 14 to 16 minutes for medium, turning once. Brush both sides with glaze several times during grilling.

*Recipe courtesy of **National Live Stock & Meat Board***

FISH & SEAFOOD

The delicate smoky flavor achieved only by cooking over coals brings out the best in fish. Choose from wonderful recipes for tuna, swordfish, salmon or trout. For shellfish lovers, there are recipes for clams, shrimp, scallops—even lobster.

SALMON STEAKS IN ORANGE-HONEY MARINADE

Makes 4 servings

⅓ cup orange juice
⅓ cup soy sauce
3 tablespoons peanut or vegetable oil
3 tablespoons catsup
1 tablespoon honey
½ teaspoon ground ginger
1 clove garlic, sliced
4 salmon steaks (about 6 ounces each)

In shallow glass dish, combine all ingredients except salmon steaks. Add salmon steaks, turning to coat with marinade. Cover and refrigerate 1 hour. Drain salmon; reserve marinade. Grill salmon, on uncovered grill, over hot **Kingsford®** **briquets** 5 minutes. Carefully turn salmon steaks, brush with marinade and grill 5 minutes longer or until salmon flakes easily when tested with fork.

Salmon Steaks in Orange-Honey Marinade

GRILLED CATFISH

Makes 4 servings

    4 farm-raised catfish steaks or fillets*
    ½ teaspoon garlic salt
    ¼ teaspoon white pepper
    Grilled vegetables

Sprinkle fish with garlic salt and pepper. Lightly oil grid. Grill fish steaks, on uncovered grill, over medium-hot **Kingsford®** briquets 4 to 5 minutes per side or until fish flakes easily when tested with fork. Garnish as desired. Serve with assorted grilled vegetables.

*If grilling catfish fillets, use a wire grill basket.

Recipe courtesy of **The Catfish Institute**

FISH FILLETS WITH DILL SAUCE

Makes 2 servings

    ½ to ¾ pound mackerel, halibut, sablefish, grouper, salmon or catfish fillets
    1 tablespoon vegetable oil
    1 teaspoon chopped fresh dill *or* ½ teaspoon dried dill weed
    Generous dash hot pepper sauce
    Dill Sauce (recipe follows)

Measure fish at its thickest part to determine cooking time. In small bowl, combine oil, dill and hot pepper sauce; brush fish fillets with dill mixture. Tear off piece of heavy-duty foil large enough to hold fish; puncture foil in several places. Place fillets on perforated foil. Grill fillets on foil, on covered grill, over medium-hot **Kingsford®** briquets about 10 minutes per inch of thickness or until fish flakes easily when tested with fork, basting often with dill mixture. Serve with Dill Sauce.

DILL SAUCE

Makes about ¼ cup

    ¼ cup sour cream or plain yogurt
    1 teaspoon finely chopped fresh dill *or*
        ¼ teaspoon dried dill weed
    ¾ teaspoon white wine vinegar
    Few drops hot pepper sauce
    Salt and pepper

In small bowl, combine sour cream, dill, vinegar and hot pepper sauce; season to taste with salt and pepper. Cover and refrigerate until ready to serve to blend flavors.

Note: Recipe can be doubled.

Recipe courtesy of **National Fisheries Institute**

GRILLED FISH WITH SALSA

Makes 4 servings

    ½ cup quartered cherry tomatoes
    ½ cup cubed mango or papaya
    ¼ cup sliced green onion
    ¼ cup cubed avocado
    2 tablespoons chopped cilantro or parsley
    1 tablespoon olive or vegetable oil
    2 tablespoons lime juice
    1 teaspoon minced jalapeño pepper
    Salt and pepper
    1¼ pounds white fish fillets (ling cod, red snapper or halibut)

In small bowl, combine tomatoes, mango, onion, avocado, cilantro, oil, 1 tablespoon of the lime juice and the jalapeño pepper. Season with salt and pepper to taste; set aside. Measure fish at its thickest part to determine cooking time. Sprinkle both sides of fish with remaining 1 tablespoon lime juice and additional pepper. Lightly oil grid. Grill fillets, on covered grill, over medium-hot **Kingsford®** briquets 10 minutes per inch of thickness or until fish flakes easily when tested with fork. Garnish with additional mango or papaya slices, if desired. Serve with salsa.

LEMON SWORDFISH

Makes 4 servings

    1 tablespoon grated lemon peel
    ¾ cup fresh lemon juice
    ¾ cup olive or vegetable oil
    ¼ to ½ cup parsley, chopped
    2 tablespoons prepared horseradish
    2 cloves garlic, minced
    1 teaspoon dried thyme, crushed
    1 teaspoon salt
    ¼ teaspoon pepper
    1 bay leaf
    1½ pounds swordfish steaks

In shallow glass dish, combine all ingredients except fish. Add swordfish; turn to coat with marinade. Cover and refrigerate at least 2 hours, turning fish occasionally. Drain fish; reserve marinade. Grill swordfish, on uncovered grill, over medium-hot **Kingsford®** briquets about 7 minutes, basting lightly with marinade. Carefully turn swordfish and grill 5 to 6 minutes longer or until fish flakes easily when tested with fork, basting lightly with marinade.

Grilled Fish with Salsa

Seafood Kabobs

SEAFOOD KABOBS

Makes 6 servings

2 dozen large sea scallops
1 dozen medium shrimp, shelled and deveined
1 can (8½ ounces) whole small artichoke hearts, drained
2 red or yellow peppers, cut into 2-inch pieces
¼ cup olive or vegetable oil
¼ cup lime juice

In large bowl, combine all ingredients and toss gently. Thread scallops, shrimp, artichoke hearts and peppers alternately on skewers; reserve marinade. Lightly oil grid. Grill kabobs, on uncovered grill, over low **Kingsford®** briquets 6 to 8 minutes or until scallops turn opaque and shrimp turn pink. Turn kabobs carefully at least twice during grilling and brush with marinade.

GRILLED LOBSTER WITH SPICY SAUCE

Makes 4 servings

4 whole, live lobsters* (1 to 1½ pounds each)
¼ cup dry sherry
3 tablespoons soy sauce
2 to 3 tablespoons sugar
2 teaspoons grated fresh ginger *or* ½ teaspoon ground ginger
1 teaspoon red pepper flakes
2 cloves garlic, minced
  Butter or margarine, melted

Bring large kettle of water to boil. Plunge lobsters into water. Return water to boil; cover and simmer 3 minutes or just until lobsters turn pink. Remove lobsters; rinse under cold running water and drain. Turn lobsters, underside up, and cut through inner shell of tails to expose meat.

For spicy sauce, in small bowl, combine remaining ingredients except butter. Brush lobster shells and meaty underside with sauce, letting sauce soak into meat. Grill lobsters, meat-side up, on covered grill, over medium-hot **Kingsford®** with Mesquite charcoal briquets 13 to 15 minutes or until meat turns opaque, basting often with sauce. When lobsters are cooked, make a deep cut lengthwise in center of underside with sharp knife. Spread halves enough to remove stomach (near head) and black vein. Crack claw shells with hammer. Serve with melted butter and additional spicy sauce.

*2 pounds jumbo fresh shrimp can be substituted for lobster. Leave shell on and thread on skewers. Grill as above, reducing cooking time to 5 minutes or until shrimp turn pink.

CAJUN FISH

Makes 4 servings

1 cup butter or margarine
2 tablespoons paprika
2 teaspoons popcorn butter salt
2 teaspoons onion powder
2 teaspoons garlic powder
2 teaspoons cayenne pepper
1½ teaspoons white pepper
1½ teaspoons black pepper
1 teaspoon dried thyme, crushed
1 teaspoon dried oregano, crushed
2 pounds red snapper fillets

Heat iron skillet directly over medium-hot **Match light®** charcoal briquets at least 15 minutes. Meanwhile, in small saucepan, melt butter. In small bowl, combine remaining ingredients except fish. Brush fillets with butter; sprinkle seasoning mix evenly on both sides of fillets. Place fillets in hot skillet and ladle melted butter over fillets.* Cook about 2 minutes on each side. Serve immediately with additional melted butter for dipping.

Note: This method of grilling produces heavy smoke.

CITRUS GRILLED WHOLE FISH WITH LIME BUTTER

Makes 6 to 8 servings

1 whole fish (about 4 pounds), such as salmon, bluefish, red snapper or trout, cleaned
Vegetable oil
Pepper
1 or 2 limes, thinly sliced
1 or 2 lemons, thinly sliced
Lime Butter (recipe follows)

Rinse inside cavity of fish under cold running water; pat dry with paper toweling. Brush cavity with oil and season with pepper. Overlap alternating lime and lemon slices in cavity of fish. Measure thickness of fish at its thickest part to determine cooking time. Place fish in oiled wire grill basket. Grill fish, on covered grill, over medium-hot **Kingsford®** briquets 10 to 12 minutes per inch of thickness or until fish flakes easily when tested with fork. Turn fish halfway through cooking time. Serve with Lime Butter.

LIME BUTTER

Makes a generous ½ cup

½ cup butter or margarine, softened
1 teaspoon grated lime peel
2 to 3 tablespoons fresh lime juice
Dash salt

In bowl or food processor, combine all ingredients. Beat or process until soft and light.

*Recipe courtesy of **National Fisheries Institute***

Grilled Shrimp in Peanut Sauce

BACON-WRAPPED TUNA

Makes 6 servings

3 pounds fresh tuna
½ cup olive or vegetable oil
¼ cup lime juice
1 cup dry white wine
2 cloves garlic, crushed
1 teaspoon grated fresh ginger
6 slices bacon

Cut tuna into 6 steaks, each about 1 inch thick. Remove any skin or bone. In shallow glass dish, combine oil, lime juice, wine, garlic and ginger. Add tuna; turn to coat with marinade. Cover and refrigerate 2 hours. Drain fish; reserve marinade. Wrap 1 slice of bacon around each steak and secure with wooden pick. Lightly oil grid. Grill fish steaks, on uncovered grill, over medium-hot **Kingsford®** briquets about 10 minutes or until fish flakes easily when tested with fork. Turn once halfway through cooking time; baste often with marinade.

GRILLED SHRIMP IN PEANUT SAUCE

Makes 4 servings

¼ cup creamy peanut butter
¼ cup soy sauce
¼ cup sugar
3 cloves garlic, minced
2 tablespoons vegetable oil
1 tablespoon water
1½ pounds medium shrimp, shelled and deveined

In saucepan, combine peanut butter and 2 tablespoons of the soy sauce; blend well. Stir in remaining 2 tablespoons soy sauce, the sugar, garlic, oil and water; heat to dissolve sugar. Thread shrimp on skewers; brush with peanut sauce. Grill shrimp, on covered grill, over medium-hot **Kingsford® with Mesquite charcoal briquets** 5 to 6 minutes or until shrimp turn pink; turn once halfway through cooking time. Brush shrimp with peanut sauce before serving.

GRILLED TROUT WITH TWO SAUCES

Makes 4 servings

4 whole, cleaned trout or other small whole fish (about 12 ounces each)
Walnut Butter Sauce (recipe follows) *or*
Tarragon Cream Sauce (recipe follows)

Grill fish on well-oiled grid or in well-oiled wire grill basket, on covered grill, over medium-hot **Kingsford® with Mesquite charcoal briquets** 3 to 5 minutes or until fish flakes easily when tested with fork; turn once. Serve with Walnut Butter Sauce or Tarragon Cream Sauce.

WALNUT BUTTER SAUCE

Makes about ½ cup

½ cup chopped walnuts
½ cup butter or margarine
3 tablespoons Madeira wine

In skillet, saute walnuts in 2 tablespoons of the butter until golden and fragrant. Reduce heat and add remaining 6 tablespoons butter; stir until melted. Stir in Madeira. Serve warm.

TARRAGON CREAM SAUCE

Makes about ½ cup

¼ cup olive or vegetable oil
¼ cup whipping cream
1 tablespoon red wine vinegar
1 tablespoon finely chopped parsley
1 garlic clove, minced
½ teaspoon dried tarragon, crushed
¼ teaspoon pepper

In medium bowl, combine all ingredients; mix well with wire whisk. Serve cool.

SHELLFISH APPETIZERS

Makes 4 appetizer servings

24 clams or 32 mussels, scrubbed
4 tablespoons white wine
½ teaspoon dried thyme, crushed

For each serving, place 6 clams or 8 mussels on each of 4 pieces of heavy-duty foil. Bring up foil around shellfish and add 1 tablespoon white wine and ⅛ teaspoon thyme to each packet. Fold foil loosely around shellfish; seal edges tightly. Grill packets over medium-hot **Kingsford® briquets** about 5 minutes or until shellfish open. (Discard any shellfish that do not open.)

*Recipe courtesy of **National Fisheries Institute***

CANTONESE GRILLED SHRIMP

Makes 4 to 6 servings

1 cup soy sauce
½ cup dry white or red wine
2 tablespoons vegetable oil
4 green onions, finely chopped
2 tablespoons grated fresh ginger
2 tablespoons brown sugar
2 teaspoons red pepper flakes
2 teaspoons sesame seed
2 pounds medium shrimp, shelled and deveined

In shallow glass dish, combine all ingredients except shrimp. Add shrimp; turn to coat with marinade. Cover and refrigerate at least 2 hours, stirring occasionally. Thread shrimp on skewers; reserve marinade. Grill shrimp, on covered grill, over medium-hot **Kingsford® briquets** 6 to 8 minutes or until shrimp turn pink, basting frequently with marinade.

BARBECUED ALASKA SALMON

Makes 12 to 16 servings

2 whole Alaska salmon fillets (about 1½ pounds each)
Salt and pepper
1 teaspoon grated lemon peel
½ cup butter or margarine, melted
¼ cup fresh lemon juice
4 teaspoons grated onion
½ teaspoon hot pepper sauce

Measure fish at its thickest part to determine cooking time. Sprinkle both sides of each fillet with salt and pepper to taste. In small bowl, combine remaining ingredients; brush both sides of fillets with butter mixture. Tear off 2 pieces of heavy-duty foil large enough to hold each fillet; puncture foil in several places. Place each fillet, skin-side down, on perforated foil. Grill salmon on foil, on covered grill, over hot **Kingsford® briquets** 10 minutes per inch of thickness or until salmon flakes easily when tested with fork. Baste often with butter mixture.

*Recipe courtesy of **Alaska Seafood Marketing Institute, Salmon Division***

Grilled Trout with Two Sauces

ALL THE EXTRAS

Here you'll find everything you need to round out a great barbecue: salads, side dishes and desserts. Some recipes are traditional favorites, such as potato salad. Others offer innovative ways to grill your favorite fruits and vegetables.

GRILLED BABY VEGETABLES

Makes 4 servings

1 pound assorted baby vegetables (such as pattypan or zucchini squash, carrots, asparagus tips or red peppers)
Prepared Italian salad dressing for basting
Green onion tops (optional)

Cut larger vegetables into halves. Brush vegetables lightly with dressing. Grill vegetables over medium-hot **Kingsford® briquets** 5 to 10 minutes or until crisp-tender, turning once and basting occasionally with dressing.

To tie vegetables into bundles, blanch green onion tops in boiling water 5 seconds or until limp. Use tops as string to tie bundles together.

BARBECUED GARLIC

Makes 4 servings

1 whole head of garlic
Olive or vegetable oil for basting

Peel loose, outermost skin from garlic; brush all over with oil. Grill garlic, on covered grill, not directly over medium-hot **Kingsford® briquets** 30 to 45 minutes or until garlic cloves are very tender, basting frequently with oil. Press individual cloves between thumb and forefinger to squeeze out garlic. Serve with grilled meats or as a spread for hot fresh bread.

Barbecued Garlic, Fresh Fruit Kabobs (page 88)
and Grilled Baby Vegetables

FRESH FRUIT KABOBS

Makes 8 servings

½ cup butter or margarine, softened
⅓ cup honey
1 tablespoon chopped fresh mint *or* 1 teaspoon dried mint, crushed
1 fresh pineapple, cored, peeled and cut into 1-inch cubes
3 fresh nectarines, pears, plums or apples, cut into wedges

In small bowl, combine butter, honey and mint. Thread fruit pieces alternately on skewers. Brush kabobs with butter-honey mixture. Grill kabobs over medium-hot **Kingsford®** briquets 3 to 5 minutes or until fruit is heated through. Turn once or twice and brush with butter-honey mixture. Serve plain or with pound cake, ice cream or whipped topping, if desired.

CHEDDAR CHEESE PEARS

Makes 6 servings

3 fresh pears, peeled, cored and cut into halves *or* 1 can (29 ounces) pear halves, drained
2 teaspoons grated lemon peel
2 tablespoons fresh lemon juice
½ cup shredded Cheddar cheese (about 4 ounces)

Arrange pears on large square of heavy-duty foil. Sprinkle lemon peel and juice over pears. Fill pear halves with cheese. Fold up foil around pears; seal edges tightly. Grill packet over medium-hot **Kingsford®** briquets 15 minutes or until pears are hot and cheese is soft.

Eggplant Parmesan

GRILLED STUFFED RED PEPPER RINGS

Makes 6 servings

4 medium red peppers
1 can (12 ounces) whole kernel corn, drained
½ cup dry bread crumbs
1 egg, beaten
1 tablespoon all-purpose flour
2 tablespoons diced onion
2 tablespoons chopped parsley
1½ cups prepared Hidden Valley Ranch® Original Ranch® Salad Dressing
Salt and pepper
1 bunch fresh spinach, washed and trimmed

Cut 3 thick rings from each pepper; remove seeds. Arrange on lightly oiled piece of heavy-duty foil. In large bowl, combine corn, bread crumbs, egg, flour, onion, parsley and ¾ cup of the salad dressing; season to taste with salt and pepper. Spoon mixture into pepper rings and pack down. Fold up foil around pepper rings into a pyramid shape. Crimp edges together to seal, allowing room for heat circulation. Grill packet over medium-hot **Kingsford®** briquets about 15 minutes. Open foil to allow rings to cool. When ready to serve, line large serving plate with spinach leaves. With wide spatula, carefully transfer stuffed rings to lined plate. Serve with remaining ¾ cup salad dressing.

EGGPLANT PARMESAN

Makes 4 servings

1 eggplant (about 1¼ pounds)
½ cup olive or vegetable oil
½ teaspoon dried oregano, crushed
½ teaspoon dried rosemary, crushed
¼ teaspoon garlic powder
6 ounces sliced mozzarella or Monterey Jack cheese
1 cup freshly grated Parmesan cheese (about 4 ounces)
1 jar (15 ounces) marinara sauce

Slice eggplant crosswise into ½-inch slices. In small bowl, combine oil, oregano, rosemary and garlic powder. Brush sides of eggplant with oil baste. Cut mozzarella cheese into slices to fit eggplant slices. Grill eggplant, on covered grill, over medium-hot **Kingsford®** with Mesquite charcoal briquets 5 minutes, turning often and brushing with baste. Arrange cheese slices on eggplant; spoon Parmesan cheese over each. Grill until cheese melts. Heat marinara sauce in small saucepan on edge of grill. Spoon hot sauce over eggplant slices before serving.

Peach Walnut Spice Cake and Insalata Rustica

PEACH WALNUT SPICE CAKE

Makes 6 to 8 servings

½ cup butter or margarine
½ cup granulated sugar
½ cup packed dark brown sugar
4 eggs
⅓ cup molasses
1 large fresh peach, chopped (about 1 cup)
2½ cups all-purpose flour
½ cup walnuts, chopped
2 teaspoons ground cinnamon
¾ teaspoon baking soda
½ teaspoon ground nutmeg
½ teaspoon salt
1 large fresh peach, cut into thin slices
Whipped cream

In large mixer bowl, cream butter and sugars until light and fluffy. Beat in eggs, then molasses. Stir in chopped peach. In medium bowl, combine flour, walnuts, cinnamon, baking soda, nutmeg and salt; stir into creamed mixture. Pour into greased and floured 9-inch square baking pan. Bake in 350°F oven 40 to 50 minutes or until wooden pick inserted in center comes out clean. Cut into squares and top with peach slices and whipped cream.

*Recipe courtesy of **California Tree Fruit Agreement***

INSALATA RUSTICA

Makes 6 servings

1 head iceberg lettuce, torn
1 head romaine lettuce, torn
1 bunch watercress, stems removed, leaves torn
2 tomatoes, sliced
6 radishes, sliced
2 large fresh peaches, cut into wedges (about 2 cups)
Mustard Dressing (recipe follows)

Arrange lettuce and watercress leaves in large salad bowl. Arrange tomatoes, radishes and peaches on top. Drizzle with Mustard Dressing.

MUSTARD DRESSING

Makes about 1 cup

½ cup vegetable oil
6 tablespoons white wine vinegar
8 teaspoons Dijon-style mustard
4 teaspoons minced garlic
1 teaspoon sugar

In small jar with tight-fitting lid, combine all ingredients. Shake to blend well.

*Recipe courtesy of **California Tree Fruit Agreement***

Spicy Quesadillas

CALIFORNIA CRAB SALAD

Makes 4 servings

1 package (0.4 ounce) Hidden Valley Ranch® Buttermilk Recipe Original Ranch® Salad Dressing Mix
1 cup buttermilk
1 cup mayonnaise
1 teaspoon prepared horseradish
1 tablespoon grated fresh ginger
2 cups cooked rice, chilled
4 lettuce leaves
½ pound cooked crabmeat, chilled
1 large ripe avocado, peeled and thinly sliced
½ medium cucumber, thinly sliced

In large bowl, combine salad dressing mix, buttermilk and mayonnaise. Whisk in horseradish and ginger. Cover and refrigerate at least 30 minutes. On serving plate, arrange rice on lettuce leaves. Arrange crabmeat, avocado slices and cucumber slices on top of rice. Garnish with lime wedges and cherry tomato, if desired. Serve with salad dressing on the side.

GRILLED DESSERT PEACHES

Makes 4 to 6 servings

3 cups sliced, peeled fresh peaches *or* 1 can (29 ounces) sliced peaches, drained
3 tablespoons almond-flavored liqueur
2 tablespoons brown sugar
    Dash ground nutmeg

Arrange peaches in lightly oiled foil pan. Sprinkle remaining ingredients over peaches. Cover pan tightly with foil. Place pan on grill over medium-hot **Kingsford® briquets** about 20 minutes or until hot.

HOT FRUIT COMPOTE

Makes 6 to 8 servings

1 can (16 ounces) pear halves, drained
1 can (20 ounces) pineapple chunks, drained
1 can (16 ounces) peach halves, drained
¼ cup butter or margarine, melted
½ cup packed brown sugar
½ teaspoon ground cinnamon

Combine all ingredients in foil pan. Place pan on grill over medium-hot **Kingsford® briquets** 20 to 25 minutes or until fruit is heated through. Stir often, spooning butter-sugar mixture over fruit while grilling.

SPICY QUESADILLAS

Makes 8 to 10 appetizer servings

½ cup chopped fresh tomatoes
⅓ cup K.C. Masterpiece® Barbecue Sauce (Spicy or Original)
⅔ cup sliced green onions
2 tablespoons lime or lemon juice
1 tablespoon red wine vinegar
1 tablespoon minced jalapeño peppers or
    2 tablespoons diced green chili peppers
    Hot pepper sauce
2 cups shredded Muenster or Monterey Jack cheese (about 8 ounces)
8 flour tortillas (6-inch)
    Vegetable oil for frying

In small bowl, combine tomatoes, barbecue sauce, 3 tablespoons of the onions, the lime juice, vinegar and jalapeño peppers. Season to taste with hot pepper sauce. Combine cheese with remaining onions. For each quesadilla, sprinkle about ½ cup cheese-onion mixture over 1 tortilla. Spoon 2 tablespoons sauce mixture over cheese; top with another tortilla, pressing gently. Fry in skillet in small amount of hot oil until golden and cheese has melted, turning once. Cut into 6 or 8 wedges. Repeat with remaining ingredients. Garnish with additional green onions, if desired. Heat remaining sauce mixture and serve with quesadillas for dipping.

California Crab Salad